SO-AWT-985

PRAYER WITH
NO INTERMISSION

⊸⊸o⌒⌒o⊸

40 DAYS TO UNCEASING PRAYER

Bill Elliff

Graceful Truth Series
Volume III

PRAYER WITH NO INTERMISSION: 40 Days to Unceasing Prayer
By Bill Elliff

Graceful Truth Series | Volume 3

Published by TruthINK Publications
6600 Crystal Hill Road
North Little Rock, Arkansas 72118

© 2018 by Bill Elliff

All rights reserved. No part of this book may be reproduced or transmitted in any form or by any means, electronic or mechanical, including photocopying and recording, or by any information storage and retrieval system, without permission in writing from the publisher.

Cover Design | Keith Runkle

ISBN-13: 978-0-9831168-4-4
ISBN-10: 0-9831168-4-9

Printed in the United States of America

Scripture Quotations taken from the New American Standard Bible Updated, Copyright © 1960, 1962, 1963, 1968, 1971, 1972, 1973, 1975, 1977, 1995 by The Lockman Foundation. Used by permission. (www.Lockman.org), *unless otherwise noted.*

Dedicated to my big sister, Sandy Smith

*Who took up our Mother's prayer mantle after her death
and is praying us through.*

Before you begin ...

What would your life be like if you could remain in the presence of God all day long? If you could pray without ceasing? If each day was a running conversation with the God-Who-Loves-Perfectly-And-Sees-All?

Even a cursory glance at the life of Jesus, both earthly and heavenly, reveals a life of continued intercession. Unceasing prayer. We know that our lives would be far more effective if this was our habit, but many don't think it's possible.

God desires for us to talk with Him all day long! His desire for us is not merely greater effectiveness, but continuous communion with Him. His love longs for unceasing prayer from those He's created.

You *can* pray without ceasing! If it were not so, God would not have called you to such a life. This simple book is designed to help you get there. I would encourage you, as you read, to *pray deeply* about your prayer life and the prayer lives of those you serve with in the kingdom. Put down the book when God speaks to you ... *and pray*! Don't let your reading be merely educational, but experiential.

Seek to discover, these next 40 days, the joy of talking with Christ about everything, all day long. He's more interested in every detail than you can imagine, and nothing is beyond His power.

Bill Elliff
Little Rock, Arkansas
May 2018

A free, downloadable, six-week video curriculum for personal
or small group use with *Prayer with No Intermission*
is available at www.billelliff.org under "RESOURCES."

This resource features six, 15-minute video lessons by Bill Elliff
and a Leader's Guide with discussion questions
and prayer guides.

DAY 1

PRAYER WITH NO INTERMISSION

Pray without ceasing.

(1 THESSALONIANS 5:17)

IT BOTHERED ME for years. Right in the middle of Paul's very practical list of admonitions is this simple, three-word command. Our tendency is to gloss over this very direct phrase, but these words form life's most important door.

Most look at this command and walk away, feeling it is unattainable. But a perfect God cannot demand of us something that we are unable to do, by His grace.

Unceasing prayer! We talk about prayer, know we should pray, encourage others to pray, but don't pray. We fail to understand that the Word of God and prayer are God's primary means of communion with Him. Prayer is opening the door to Christ, letting Him into our needs. It is being with Him. It is humility, for real prayer is admitting our failures and weakness. It is faith, because it is acknowledging a Source beyond ourselves.

Apparently, God thinks we need to pray with no intermission.

1

GOD CALLING

All of life is a process by God to restore what was lost in Eden. God is bringing us back to Himself. The whole work of Christ is aimed at this blessed reality. When we realize this and are drawn to Him, we are saved from sin and death and hell. But salvation is so much more than merely legal pardon. It opens the way for an ongoing, intimate relationship with Jesus.

Prayer is to be the running dialogue we are now offered with the God of the universe and His Son who loves us with perfect, unceasing passion. It is not merely one of the things we do as a follower of Christ. It is a description of the atmosphere in which we can now live. The life-giving air we can now breathe.

We often shy away from prayer or ignore it altogether, but we must realize that prayer is not just about us, it is for Him. The Father wants to be with His children, just as you long to be with your earthly family.

GOD WORKING

There are things that God plans to do through no other means but prayer. He reminds us of this continually in order to bring us back into constant communion with Him. He not only invites us, He makes outlandish promises:

- *"Everything you pray for, believing you will receive!"* (Matthew 21:22)

- *"The effective, fervent prayer of a righteous man will accomplish much!"* (James 5:16)

- *"Whatever you ask in My name I will do it so that the Father may be glorified in the Son. If you ask for anything in My name, I will do it."* (John 14:13)

- *"Until now you asked for nothing in My name; ask and you will receive so that your joy may be full."* (John 16:24)

It sounds too amazing to be true. It is the invitation of a Father intent upon bringing us to Himself. But prayer without ceasing? This is the fantastical part. We can imagine ourselves praying occasionally. Praying when there is an urgent crisis. Praying when we need heavenly fire trucks to rush to our aid. But, without ceasing? With no intermission?

GOD SPEAKING

God is talking all the time. He is not silent, but there are few who get quiet enough to hear Him. There are few who listen.

All around you right now are radio waves filled with music and talk. They are loud and incessant, but you walk through your day, blissfully ignorant of their presence. If, though, you turn on a radio receiver and dial into the right channel, you will immediately realize that this communication has been going on all along. It was there, waiting for you.

GOD PRESENT

God is here. You can leave the receiver dialed to Him constantly and hear the dialogue of His love, encouragement, and direction. To go there means you must lay down other voices and distractions and give Him your attention. You must tune away from every idol and loud, competing voice. He is here, but He will not be heard if you do not refuse the noise around you. (This is one of the great values of fasting from the incessant voices of the world. Your soul is humbled and quieted by a refusal of the world's noise. In the quietness, God can be heard in exquisite ways.)

You must do whatever is necessary to listen for His voice. And, it must be highly intentional, fueled by a deep understanding of your spiritual poverty and need. You must pray, not just with a bowed head or bended knee, but with a heart that is gladly tuned to Him throughout every moment of the common day. You must realize that prayer is not a part of the Christ-life, it is the Christ-life, and you must sacrifice everything to still each competing voice.

If you do, you will find the sweetest, most intimate words that a human can experience. You will be surprised at its refreshment and joy. Amazed at its consistency. Stunned that it is so personal. Awed by how perfectly God knows exactly what you need to hear, every second of the day. And, you will wonder why you have waited so long to pray without ceasing.

Pray it in: Would you pray the following prayer for the next 40 days (and beyond): "*Lord, would you make me a man/woman of unceasing prayer?*" God has everything to gain by answering this prayer!

DAY 2

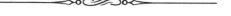

THE ALL OF PRAYER

*Praying at **all** times in the Spirit, with **all** prayer and supplication. To that end keep alert with **all** perseverance, making supplication for **all** the saints.*

(EPHESIANS 6:18, emphasis mine)

ONE OF THE great quests of the spiritually maturing Christian is non-stop communion with God. Can we go a day without ever leaving the presence of Christ? Every thought captured by Him? Every conversation including Him as a very present voice? Outer ears tuned to others, inner ears tuned to Christ? Never losing the sense of His presence?

Surely for a day. And if a day, then a week. And if a week, then a month and a year. Like a runner pushing to greater and greater distances, can we give the same focus to that which is most essential to our souls and others? The ALL of prayer.

Apparently, Paul had experienced this and believed we could too. To put a stamp on this thought, Paul pounds it into our thinking with the four "all's" that condition our prayers.

ALL TIMES

There should never be a day when we are not praying. Ever. There is not a spot where communion with God is not appropriate. If we find prayer needless, awkward, or embarrassing, it may be that we are new at communing with God or we have forgotten its necessity. Or, the press of the world has distracted us and pulled us away from simple, pure communion with the One our soul desperately needs.

It could be that we have forgotten how much God Himself longs for our fellowship—not out of need, but out of the perfection of His love. He calls us to pray at all times.

ALL PRAYER

What kind of communication do you have with your best friend? Is it always the same? All joy, but no sorrow? All gut-wrenching confession, but no happy celebration of victories? All about the weather, nothing about the kids? The great joy of a real friend is the all-ness of your speech. No holds barred, no subject off limits; mutual sharing of anything and everything. Intimacy is gained with a good friend through all-ness.

Should it be less with God? God wants to be included in your most stunning moments and most routine. He wants you to acknowledge Him in your greatest successes, and turn to Him—not run away from Him—in the valleys of your greatest failures. He longs to be in your thoughts and He has profound and precise things to say to you about everything in your life. And sometimes, He wants nothing more than to sit by the fire with you in simple fellowship and affirming love. All types of communication, all the time.

ALL PERSEVERANCE

This is the great downfall. We give up. Encouraged by a sermon or a scripture, we jump into moments of prayer, but we fail to persevere. We get tired or distracted—"worried and bothered by so many things," like Martha, when "only one thing is necessary," like Mary.

If we are going to be robust Christians for God, we must be great pray-ers. And, if we are going to be great pray-ers, we must become obstinate in our refusal to walk away from the table with Him. We must pray and *keep praying*, all the time. When we realize our lapse, we must repent and return (and keep returning) until there is a long obedience in the right direction.

> *"There is no power like that of prevailing prayer—of Abraham pleading for Sodom, Jacob wrestling in the stillness of the night, Moses standing in the breach, Hannah intoxicated with sorrow, David heartbroken with remorse and grief, Jesus in sweat and blood. Add to this list from the records of the church your personal observation and experience, and always there is cost of passion unto blood. Such prayer prevails. It turns ordinary mortals into men of power. It brings power. It brings fire. It brings rain. It brings life. It brings God."*
> *(Samuel Chadwick)*

ALL THE SAINTS

Who needs our prayers? Everyone we know and even those we don't know! We should pray for those we love and those with whom we struggle. Even our enemies, Jesus said (and illustrated) should be the recipients of our intercession. Government leaders and waiters at our table.

Don't you imagine that Jesus talked with His Father constantly about each of the disciples and everyone He met—receiving continual instruction about how he was to interact with them and intercede for their needs?

His testimony was that He did nothing on His own initiative but only said what His Father was saying and did what He observed His Father doing. What was the vehicle for this observation of the Father? Constant prayer in every situation. Jesus lifted everything vertically, looking up to ask what should be done and interceding for what could be done. Every sweep of Christ's eyes across the landscape of humanity led Him to intercede.

Prayer should not be our last resort with people, but our first response. Is there anyone we will meet today who does not need what God could bring them through our prayers? If we could master the ALL of prayer, we would find the foyer of heaven and the power of God on earth. His kingdom would come and His will done on earth as it is being done in heaven. And, our Father would have gained the communion with His children that He desires.

Pray it in: How is your prayer life on a scale of 1-10? What "ALL" is missing? Ask God, right now, to build this into your prayer life in the next 40 days.

DAY 3

NIGHT AND DAY

And there was a prophetess, Anna the daughter of Phanuel, of the tribe of Asher. She was advanced in years and had lived with her husband seven years after her marriage, and then as a widow to the age of eighty-four. She never left the temple, serving night and day with fastings and prayers. At that very moment she came up and began giving thanks to God and continued to speak of Him to all those who were looking for the redemption of Jerusalem.

(LUKE 2:36-39)

SOME MUST HAVE thought her strange. The aged widow, Anna, had virtually lived in the temple for decades. She served there, and her serving was amplified by continual fasting and unceasing prayer.

On a normal day—one of thousands for her—she was going about her routine in prayer and sensed an unusual presence. No doubt the atmosphere seemed strangely electrified.

Simeon, another temple regular, had the eyes to see because he had also sought the Messiah for years. Gazing upon a young, 40-day-old baby, his heart was moved by the Spirit to announce that this was the Messiah for whom they had been waiting. Only God could have made him aware of this phenomena.

Anna instantly knew. The Messiah, of whom the temple was merely a picture, had come.

SHE NEVER LEFT

... is the amazing phrase. Something in Anna's heart caused her to continue in prayer. It was not merely her daytime routine. She prayed "night and day." There could be no question that there were many other things she could have done. But something—or rather, Someone—kept drawing her back to the place of prayer.

Anna could have refused those promptings, but thankfully for us, she did not.

THE REWARD OF PREVAILING PRAYER

Prayer is not directionless. God has agendas for us in prayer, both immediate and eternal. He is always taking us somewhere when we are intentionally pursuing Him in prayer.

Anna had been praying, and the Lord had been preparing her and the world around her for the greatest manifestation of God's presence in human history. "The Word became flesh and dwelt among us and we saw His glory" (John 1:14).

His coming involved preparation. It called for believing people to cooperate with God to prepare a highway for the Messiah. Only heaven will unveil to us what was being accomplished through Anna's decades of believing prayer. Perhaps it was to make her so familiar with God that she would recognize Him when He came. It gave her eyes to see. Perhaps it was to prepare a whole generation to see. Perhaps it was for us to see.

Anna persevered in prayer and was one of the fortunate ones who saw Christ in human flesh. Her prayers paved the way for His coming.

People who pray have a heightened sense of God. Because they are with God daily, hourly in prayer, when He manifests Himself they are instantly aware that it is Him. Conversely, they know when Christ is not present—even when others claim that He is.

Anna was privileged to live for years in the place closest to the Throne, and then to see and instantly recognize and rejoice in the physical answer to her prayers.

She prayed night and day. And so must we.

Pray it in: Begin praying every morning before you get out of bed and every night as you go to bed ... even if it's just for a few minutes.

DAY 4

THE FUEL OF DESPERATION

IT IS TRAGIC that we often do not cry out in prayer until we have exhausted all other possibilities. We know that we are growing in prayer when we advance beyond mere "crisis praying." When our love for intimacy with Christ, our passion for people without Him, and our belief that God can change things through prayer leads us to unceasing intercession.

For most, prayer is fueled by desperation. And, there is a sense in which our prayers should never lose this urgency.

PERSISTENT PRAYER

In Luke 18, God recounts two stories that challenge us to increased prayer. First, the persistent widow who wore the unrighteous judge out so that he finally agreed to do what she asked. Jesus gave the following commentary on her persistence:

> *And will not God give justice to his elect, who cry to him day and night? Will he delay long over them? I tell you, he will give justice to them speedily. Nevertheless, when the Son of Man comes, will he find faith on earth?"*
> *(Luke 18:7-8 ESV)*

God is looking for people who will pray and not faint. The problem we have is not His unwillingness to answer, but our unwillingness to persevere in incessant prayer. He indicates that He will "give justice to [persistent pray-ers] speedily." But He then asks this question of us, "When He comes, will He find faith on earth?"

In other words, He will do His part in the prayer equation with perfect timing and precision, but will we do our part? Will He find us trusting Him? Looking to Him? Crying out to Him in dependency and expectancy? Praying unceasingly? Will He find us so overwhelmed by the needs around us, and so believing in His prayer receptivity and powerful faithfulness, that we will not give up in prayer?

INCREASED PRAYER

At the close of Luke, Chapter 18, is the account of another desperate pray-er—a blind beggar. When he heard that Jesus was passing by, he cried out for mercy. When other people tried to silence him, he "cried out all the more."

His desperation made him shameless. He must have thought Jesus was his only hope. He must have believed that Jesus could actually change his life. And, he must have known that his opportunity was fleeting.

Jesus hears cries like this, and he described the blind man's desperate cry with one word: faith. When faced with external pressure to quit praying, this man's belief in Jesus caused him to *increase* his cry.

An African pastor once said to one of my friends, "In our country, we did not cry out to God until there came destruction.

I wonder when the American church will turn and cry out to God? Will it be at the point of desperation or destruction?"

God is looking for people of persistent, desperate faith. Faith is the key that unlocks the door and makes room for God. And faith expresses itself in desperate cries.

Prayer that will never give up. Prayer that cries out *all the more.*

Pray it in: What are you desperate for God to do? Write these desperate prayers down and begin to pray over them daily.

DAY 5

CHRIST'S HABITS AND OURS

As was His custom ...

(LUKE 22:39)

THERE ARE MANY things that have become habitual to us. If you think about your morning routine, you will discover that you usually do the exact same thing in the same way each day. Such habits are always developed by a devotion to something we consider valuable—something important to our day.

It would be important, then, to understand what the Perfect Man's habits were. It would make sense that His routines were exactly as ours should be. And, as you study the life of Jesus, one habit stands out above all the rest.

*And He came out and proceeded **as was His custom** to the Mount of Olives; and the disciples also followed Him. When He arrived at the place, He said to them, "Pray that you may not enter into temptation." And He withdrew from them about a stone's throw, and knelt down and **began to pray**, saying, Father, if You are willing, remove this cup from Me;*

15

yet not My will, but Yours be done."

Now an angel from heaven appeared to him, strength-ening Him. **And being in agony He was praying very fervently**; *and His sweat became like drops of blood, falling down upon the ground.*

When He **rose from prayer**, *He came to the disciples and found them sleeping from sorrow, and said to them, "Why are you sleeping? Get up and* **pray that you may not enter into temptation.***" (Luke 22:39-46, emphasis mine)*

Jesus' habit was to retire to His place of prayer and pray. When the disciples were sorrowful, they slept. When Jesus was sorrowful, He prayed. To Him, prayer was the foundation and the pathway of life and ministry. It was not secondary. How else could He find and do His Father's will if He was not in communion with heaven?

PRAYING ABOUT TEMPTATION
Twice Jesus told His disciples the antidote for temptation was prayer. We are all going to be tempted, but if you do not want to "enter into" temptation, you must pray. Prayer will open your eyes to see temptation for what it is—a diabolical design to destroy you and abort God's kingdom. And prayer will give you the Divine strength to overcome it when it comes.

PRAYING ABOUT SERVICE
Jesus' habit also illustrated the perfect posture we must assume when we are asked by God to take a hard path ... a path that calls for great submission to the Father's will.

We must pray.

Jesus shows us it is perfectly legitimate to ask God to remove us from such trials, but also that they should be approached with a predisposition of surrender. This all occurred for Jesus when He was talking to the One who knew Him best and loved Him most. The One whose will is good, acceptable, and perfect.

Notice that when Jesus prayed, God dispatched an angel from heaven to give Him the strength that He needed to face the mission ahead. Will He not do the same for us, giving us the empowerment for every task He assigns ... *if we pray*?

PREPARED IN PRAYER

Jesus "rose from prayer" and went straight toward the task. His disciples were not prepared for what was to come, but Christ was. Why? He had prayed, "*as was His custom.*"

We will face much today. Temptations will come our way. Opportunities for ministry will be all around us. Divine strength will be desperately needed. It will be our *custom of prayer* that will prepare us for every challenge and opportunity.

Will we be ready?

Pray it in: Would you ask God to begin to awaken you for prayer, and to give you such an understanding of the value of this time that you will quickly cooperate with Him, whenever He calls you to communion with Him? Would you ask Him to help you develop a new habit in prayer?

DAY 6

THE ONE PLACE YOU MUST BE STRONG

Be devoted to prayer, keeping alert in it with an attitude of thanksgiving.

(COLOSSIANS 4:2)

EVERY LEADER HAS strengths. Some are better communicators than others. Others are very personable, while some are wonderfully administrative. I learned a long time ago that I should cultivate the areas where I'm gifted and staff to my weaknesses as much as possible. But there are some insufficient areas that must be developed.

You are a leader, for everyone leads someone. As a leader, there is one place you cannot afford to be weak. Every spiritual leader must be *strong in prayer*.

WHAT WE MUST DO

The word "devotion" that Paul uses under the inspiration of the Spirit literally means, "be strong towards." Some people are strong towards work, others strong at sports. Some people know the characters of every movie and can quote the lines of their favorites. Some are completely devoted to computer games, spending mindless hours wasting precious God-given time.

But if God has called you to the high task of leading others, you must be strong towards prayer. There is no excuse and no substitute. People should look at you and without a second thought say, "they are very, very devoted to prayer."

WHAT PRAYER CAN DO

Why should this be our recognizable strength? Because this is the model of all those in human history who made a difference for the kingdom. And, most convincingly, the model of our Leader.

When administrative needs grew in the early church, the Apostles wisely selected godly men to put in charge of these tasks. The reason? "We will devote ourselves to prayer and the ministry of the Word" (Acts 6:4). Notice the order. Prayer is first and equal in importance to the Word of God.

Effective leaders understand that prayer can do what God can do. Prayer is our singular path to bring God into every realm of ministry to others. Prayer is the key to God's presence and power resting on our lives and the lives of others. Prayer is always the precursor to revival. (Can you imagine God bringing revival to a prayerless people? Spiritual awakening can always be traced back to the mercy of God in response to some praying individual or group).

Prayerlessness is the worst sin because it is the highest indication of pride. A day without prayer is a day we've told God we can live without Him. It speaks of a lack of trust and the vain work of human ability alone. How can we hope to know God's agenda? Lead people where they need to go? Give them what

God is saying? See God's power resting on those we are called to lead? See real life change in us and others?

OUR HIGHEST PRAYER

Paul says we must "pray without ceasing." I long for that continuity. It is my great prayer that those three words would someday be said of me. That people would remark, "Well, he is not this nor that, but he prays all the time. Our pastor walks in the presence of the Lord. He constantly breathes the oxygen of heaven ... and he leads us there. And when he says something or leads us somewhere, we know it is initiated by God."

If you are not good at prayer, cry out. Pray until you are a better intercessor. Get around people who pray. Find a regular, weekly prayer partner and learn together. Call together a dozen people and work diligently at your most important task. Read books on prayer. Study and memorize the prayers of the Scripture, which will dramatically help you in your praying.

If you are desperate for prayer, God will exponentially help you in your pursuit. He knows that prayerlessness is the one weakness you cannot afford as you lead people for whom He died.

Pray it in: Ask God today to give you some prayer partners. See the Appendix at the end of the book for some other books to read to build your prayer life this year. Determine before God in prayer to make this a year of great advance in your prayer life.

DAY 7

WHAT MAKES GOD
HEAR ME IN PRAYER?

*In the days of His flesh, He offered up both prayers and
supplications with loud crying and tears to the One
able to save Him from death, and He was heard
because of His piety.*

(HEBREWS 5:7)

DOES GOD HEAR everyone's prayer? Surely, as an all-knowing
God, He is capable of hearing everyone. But, apparently there
are some prayers to which He gives lesser attention. Jesus, our
ultimate example, was always heard by His Father, and the writer
of Hebrews tells us why.

GOD'S GROUND RULES IN PRAYER
There are some conditions to prayer. One is desperation, with
the humility that is borne out of our recognition of need. But
further, God hears and answers the prayers of those who are
willing to humbly obey as He instructs. Why would He answer
our prayers if He knows we have no intention of obeying Him?

Jesus was heard "because of his piety." We do not, and cannot, be sinless like Christ. But there should be in us a heart's disposition to follow Him as faithfully as we can by His grace.

For instance, let's say your son not only wants a car, but he needs a car for transportation and he asks you for this provision. But, he has repeatedly violated the use of your car each time it has been entrusted to him. And he openly tells you that if he gets a car, he will use it to speed, go places where he should not go, and do things you know are harmful to him. Would you answer his pleas for a car? To do so would be less than loving. Further, to wisely withhold the provision would potentially create a desire for the car that is so great it might lead him to humbly submit to your directives about its use.

> *"Why are there such numberless unanswered prayers? ... Christ taught us that the answer depended upon certain conditions. He spoke of faith, of perseverance, of praying in His Name, of praying the will of God. But all of these conditions were summed up in the one central one: 'If you abide in Me, ask whatsoever you will and it shall be done unto you.' It became clear that the power to pray the effectual prayer of faith depended upon the life. It is only to a man given up living as entirely in Christ and for Christ as the branch in the vine and for the vine, that these promises can come true."* (Andrew Murray, "The Ministry of Intercession: A Plea for More Prayer")

GOD'S GRACE IN PRAYER

Nobody deserves God's attention. Each time He bends His ear to hear the cries of sinners saved by grace, it is an act of pure mercy and compassion. We will never be "good enough" to merit answered prayer. Always, we come to God in the name of Jesus. We come because our Elder Brother said we could come and has provided a way for us to have "peace facing God" through His blood shed for our sins (Romans 5:1-2).

But prayer is not a heavenly slot machine. It is connecting with the God of the universe. We come on His terms, not ours. We may say that we are waiting on God to answer our prayers and may even be frustrated in His slowness. It may be that God has other reasons for the delay. He is waiting because He knows it's best. He is delaying answers because things are not ready, and it is not time. But, it may be He is waiting for piety. For the reverence for Him that results in a surrendered life.

GOD'S PURPOSE IN PRAYER

God is never random in the design of His disciplines. He plans for prayer to be our means of communion with Him, but also a tool to develop us and accomplish great purposes in and through our lives. Time in His presence will change us into His likeness and fit us for His work. His conditions for prayer push us toward a life *with* Him, which leads to conformity *to* Him.

This is no game. God has a lot at stake. We cannot play around with God and expect our lives to fulfill their destiny—a destiny found through communion with Him in prayer and His Word. God needs serious men and women as His instruments to accomplish His agenda.

If we desire God's attention, we must give Him ours, not only in prayer but in a Godward life. And that application must begin *right now*.

Pray it in: Focus your prayers on confession right now. What are the areas of your life that are hindering your prayers because of unconfessed, unrepentant sin?

DAY 8

WHAT DO YOU DO
WHEN YOU ARE AFRAID?

I WAS SEVEN years old. Trying to build something with a hatchet and a 2×4 by myself was not what my father would have allowed, but my father and mother were both gone. So, I sneaked into his workshop and promptly proceeded in almost cutting my left forefinger off. With blood gushing from my finger, I thought I was going to die. I was scared to death.

My teenage sister, somewhat prone to hysteria, was at home. She called one of the other pastors on my dad's church staff and they took us to the hospital. His son was my best seven-year-old friend and he rode with us. He could see I was petrified.

"Billy," he said calmly. "Do you remember the verse we learned last week in Vacation Bible School?"

"Yes," I meekly replied, with more fear than faith. "What time I am afraid, I will trust in Thee, Psalms 56:3!" As I recited and prayed in one breath, the Lord picked me up and put me on top of His promise. As suddenly as it had come, the fear was gone. Completely. It was the first instance I can remember in my life of a trembling prayer transformed to a settled faith.

We all have moments of fear. If we don't deal with them properly, they can take us places we never planned to go. Many harmful steps have been taken (or missed) because of fear. So, how do we handle fear?

A FEAR FROM THE PAST

Jacob was fearful and had reason to be. He had deceived his brother and run away from his wrath. He now returns after many years and his scouts tell him that Esau is coming with a great army. "Then Jacob was greatly afraid and distressed" (Genesis 32:7). Jacob's response? He prayed!

> *Jacob said, "O God of my father Abraham and God of my father Isaac, O Lord, who said to me, 'Return to your country and to your relatives, and I will prosper you,' I am unworthy of all the lovingkindness and of all the faithfulness which You have shown to Your servant; for with my staff only I crossed this Jordan, and now I have become two companies.*
>
> *"Deliver me, I pray, from the hand of my brother, from the hand of Esau; for I fear him, that he will come and attack me and the mothers with the children. For You said, 'I will surely prosper you and make your descendants as the sand of the sea, which is too great to be numbered.'"* (Genesis 32:9-12)

Dissect the prayer and you will find it incredibly instructive. Jacob reminded God that He had led him to return to his own country. Jacob is on this particular path because of God's initiation, and Jacob knew that where God initiates He protects and provides.

Jacob humbly admits his unworthiness and cries out for deliverance. He realizes that only God can protect him. He takes his fear right to the throne of the Lion of the Tribe of Judah.

But the clincher is found in verse 12 as Jacob reminds God of His promises. "For you said," Jacob prays. "You made a promise, Lord, and I am trusting in Your faithfulness." Obviously, Jacob remembered God's Word. He overcomes his fear by rehearsing and resting on the promises of God through prayer.

THERE'S PLENTY FOR YOU

There are 7,000 promises from God to us in the Bible. They are given for our direction, but also for our comfort. They are there for us today and every day. These promises, combined with our faith and prayer, are God's operating system with man. God longs for us to turn to Him instantly in prayer when we are fearful or distressed. And, to take Him at His word.

Joseph Scriven was born in Scotland in 1820 and later migrated to Canada. He was engaged to be married and the preparations had been made. Tragically, his wife drowned days before the wedding. Scriven found his solace in God's Word and prayer. Out of that experience he penned these words:

What a friend we have in Jesus! All our sins and grief to bear.
What a privilege to carry everything to Him in prayer.
Oh, what peace we often forfeit. Oh, what needless pain we bear,
All because we do not carry everything to God in prayer.

Are you worried about anything this week or in this season of your life? You will either try to manage it yourself, resulting in fear and distress, or go to God and His Word in unceasing prayer, resting in faith on the promises of God.

Pray it in: Write down your three greatest fears. Ask God to show you three great promises that address those fears. Write them down beside your fears and **pray it in**!

D A Y 9

FIXER UPPER

ONE OF THE most popular television series, as I write this, is a home improvement show by Chip and Joanna Gaines. They take the "worst house in the best neighborhood" and restore it to its original purpose. It begins with an inspection, and what they usually find is disastrous.

HEAVENLY INSPECTION

Jesus did such an inspection as He came into the holy city, Jerusalem.

> *Jesus entered Jerusalem and came into the temple; and after looking around He left for Bethany with the twelve, since it was already late. (Mark 11:11)*

Don't miss the seemingly random bit of travelogue: "after looking around." The Wuest Expanded translation says it like this: "After giving everything a comprehensive inspection."

Jesus never did anything randomly. What was He inspecting? The answer becomes clear the next day.

Then they came to Jerusalem. And He entered the temple and began to drive out those who were buying and selling in the temple, and overturned the tables of the money changers and the seats of those who were selling doves; and He would not permit anyone to carry merchandise through the temple. And He began to teach and say to them, "Is it not written, 'My house shall be called a house of prayer for all the nations?' But you have made it a robber's den." (Mark 11:15-18)

It was His house! Jesus was making an inspection to see what was happening in the very home He had designed. When He reported to His Father what was happening, and received instructions from the Architect and Builder of the temple, He came back the next day and cleaned house.

OUR HOUSE

He still inspects His house. Look at Revelation, Chapters 3-4, and you will see Jesus, after his ascension, returning to the seven churches and telling them what to do to clean up the church. He has the authority to do so and we should be grateful for His intense interest.

We should be aware that He is looking at our churches all the time. It is His body. Just as we examine our body if there is a problem, so does He.

What does He find as He "looks around at everything" in our churches? Vain worship? Holy, sacred things being used for selfish, secular purposes? His mission being ignored? His presence not sought?

And, most importantly, is our church missing its essential task—to be a house of prayer for all nations? Is prayer foundational to all we do, or relegated to a small closet for the few who are interested? Does He find us doing, with what is His, what He desires?

It's time to ruthlessly and relentlessly clean house. It is past time to make His house a house of prayer.

Pray it in: Pray for your church, and the churches of your city by name. Ask God to do a supernatural, transforming work to make them houses of prayer for all the nations.

DAY 10

OVERCOMING TEMPTATIONS THROUGH PRAYER

Pray that you do not enter into temptation.

(Luke 22:40)

EVERYBODY IS TEMPTED. Jesus was no exception. He was "tempted in all points like we are, yet without sin." We will never be free from temptation, but how do we overcome the constant pull of the world, the flesh, and the devil? Is it possible to not "enter in" to temptation? To resist? Is there a pill we can take? A step that will help us and help others?

Jesus' prescription? Pray. And immediately following this statement, that's exactly what He did.

JESUS' GREATEST TEMPTATION

... was to run from the horrendous suffering of the cross. Satan from the beginning had tempted Christ to take an alternate route.

Jesus, when tempted, "knelt down and began to pray." He asked the Father if He could be spared from the cup of suffering He was about to drink. No doubt there was the temptation to run from the task assigned. To yield to the "lust of the eyes and the lust of the flesh and the boastful pride of life." To compromise and take the path of least resistance. To ignore the cross in selfishness.

These were the enormous temptations that He must have faced. We do not know the particulars, but we do know that the temptation was so great He had to agonize in prayer. He knew the only remedy against this temptation was to linger in the presence of the Father in earnest conversation. He needed to hear God's instructing voice again so His will could be rightly aligned to the will of the Father.

The key to this prayer was the final sentence: "Yet not my will, but Yours be done." The bent will is the posture necessary for believers to resist all temptation. But notice ... this bent will came as the result of a bent knee. Prayer brought fresh surrender into the situation.

And, prayer worked for Jesus. Jesus did not enter into temptation and we are all eternally grateful.

WHY PRAY?

Most of us think prayer is a matter of getting God to do what we want so He will give us what we think we need. But the greatest purpose of prayer is to come into the presence of the Father and align our will with His. To let Heaven re-adjust our plan to God's perfect, sovereign plan.

Such praying is our best antidote to temptation. We may ask that God alleviate some of the temptation and He can. But we will, like Jesus, face extraordinary temptations in our daily lives. Our greatest prayer should be that we would not "enter into" temptation—to indulge, latch on. This should be our constant, daily prayer.

Can you imagine what this week would be like if we never entered into the temptations before us? The temptations were there, but we consistently bent the knee in prayer and bent our will to His will? How effective we would become! How clearly we would hear God! What leadership and witness we could give to others! What a testimony we would have of the power of answered prayer!

Pray it in: Where do you need to bend your will to the will of God? Wrestle with God in prayer about this today until you have submitted to His will ... and then, go meet the day!

DAY 11

5 THINGS GOD WANTS
TO SAY TO YOU

Pray without ceasing.

(1 THESSALONIANS 5:17)

GOD IS THE God of more. He longs for us to grant Him access to our lives through the continuing posture of unceasing prayer. The Lord has some things to say to you that will help you see the inestimable value of such a life—to forever change the way you view the privilege of prayer. If you were to sit with Him and ask "Lord, what do you want to say to me personally about prayer?" what would He say? Based on things He's already said in His Word, we can imagine the conversation might go something like this ...

#1
I WANT YOU TO KNOW THAT I AM WAITING FOR YOU

I am more interested in prayer than you are, because I am more complete in my love than you are. If you loved like I love, you would want to talk with Me without ceasing. Unceasing prayer is not a command, but an invitation! And, I long for you to long for Me. I do not want to be shut out, to be ignored, or to not be consulted, for I know that there is so much more for you in My kingdom if you will pray without ceasing. (*1 Thessalonians 5:17*)

#2

I WANT YOU TO KNOW THAT PRAYER IS NOT COMPLICATED

It is the heart of humble helplessness that looks to Me, not to yourself. This is faith. Your greatest qualification for prayer without ceasing is your *helplessness.* The more helpless you are, the more qualified you are to pray. I am knocking at the door, desiring entrance. I am longing for you to open the door and grant Me access to your greatest areas of helplessness, all day long. To pray is to let Me in. (*Revelation 3:20*)

#3

I WANT YOU TO LEARN THE ART OF RETIRING INTO ME

... to learn how to stop, listen, and be silent throughout the day. It is the art of listening that makes My voice clear and distinct. I want you to learn how to quiet your soul in the midst of anything and everything. To abide in Me. Some of this is external: resisting the noise of the world. Some is internal: practicing the presence of God. Retreating. Consciously listening, for I am here and I am not silent. (*John 15:4-5*)

#4

I WANT YOU TO ASK MORE OF ME IN PRAYER, SO YOUR JOY WOULD BE FULL!

Until now, you have asked for nothing. Ask and you will receive so your joy may be full. As you do, the world will see Me. I want to use you to show the world—and I want to use your church to show the world—that I answer the prayers of My people. That I am here constantly, waiting for them to pray. (*John 15:11*)

#5

I WANT YOUR LIFE TO BEAR GREAT, LASTING FRUIT

I have so much more for you than you can imagine! You are fearfully and wonderfully made. I have given you spiritual gifts. My very Self, the Holy Spirit, resides in you. I will guide you into great prayers if you will listen to Me, and I will produce great fruit through you if you will surrender and obey My promptings. I want to produce fruit through you that will last into eternity. But ... you must pray! (*John 15:16*)

Pray it in: Walk carefully through all five of these Biblical thoughts again. Would you pause right now and respond in prayer to each of these things He is saying to you?

DAY 12

THE PRAYER THAT NEVER FAILS

THIS WEEK AND this year each of us will face many different experiences. Problems will arise, burdens will come. Decisions will need to be made and many are life-altering. You might be facing some today. If not today, then soon.

What will we do? If we are serious followers of Jesus, we know we must pray, because only prayer brings God into the middle of our circumstances. God has created us in His image. As such, we have a certain level of control. We can decide to do things without God, or prayerfully invite Him in.

If we try to handle life alone, we will quickly discover that our mere humanity will fail us.

WHAT TO PRAY?

We all want to pray effectively. No one desires to lift some flimsy, selfish prayer that accomplishes little, but the "effective, fervent prayer" that "accomplishes much," of which James 5:16 speaks.

Jesus, as always, gives us the answer for effective prayer. He models for us the perfect prayer to pray in any situation—the prayer that is always rewarded.

"Now My soul has become troubled; and what shall I say, 'Father, save Me from this hour'? But for this purpose I came to this hour. **Father, glorify Your name.**" *(John 12:27-28, emphasis mine)*

EMBRACE GOD'S PURPOSE AND PRAY ACCORDINGLY

Jesus knew that He had been sent on purpose by His Father. That He lived on mission. He came to seek and save that which had been lost—the people that the Creator made in His image who had wandered from Him. Christ came to bring them back so their lives would worship and serve their King.

When Christ came to the most significant decision in His earthly life, He did not pray, "God, remove this from Me," or, "Let me be comfortable," or, "Save me from this pain." As He faced the grueling prospect of the cross, the most effective prayer, the one that is always answered was this: "Father, glorify Your name."

God delights to answer this prayer and the results are stunning. This prayer, prayed from a humble, genuine heart, is the prayer that never fails.

Pray it in: Spend time praying and personalizing this prayer below. You might want to put it on a card and let it become a common prayer for every tough situation that you face.

"Answer my cry, O Lord, in a way that will accomplish Your will, for Your will is good, acceptable, and perfect. If it is best for You then it is best for me and any others who may be affected by this prayer. Father, I want You to be magnified and seen in this circumstance. May all that happens glorify You!"

DAY 13

IT NEVER HURTS TO ASK

WE KNOW VERY little about him in human history. A simple man who prayed a simple prayer and received a simply-wonderful answer.

There are only two verses in the Bible about the man named Jabez, but they are recorded for a very important reason.

> *Jabez was more honorable than his brothers, and his mother named him Jabez saying, "Because I bore him with pain." Now Jabez called on the God of Israel, saying, "Oh that You would bless me indeed and enlarge my border, and that Your hand might be with me, and that You would keep me from harm that it may not pain me!" And God granted him what he requested. (1 Chronicles 4:9-10)*

Recently I helped one of my kids and their family move. I was driving back from Austin, Texas, to Little Rock, Arkansas, pulling a 32' travel trailer. If you've done this, you know a Texas wind is not your friend.

I was hit, for about the tenth time, with a gust of wind south of Texarkana, Texas, that almost knocked me off the road. If a car had been in the lane next to me, we would have disastrously collided. I looked over to see a flagpole, and the flags were flying parallel to the ground. After multiple days of work, great tiredness, semi-trucks all around, and construction zones every few miles, I was gripping the wheel.

As I stopped for gas, I asked the Lord, "Father, I know you don't have to do this, but could you let the wind die down, or, if not, just keep my trailer from being so hard to handle, I would be so grateful. But, as always, glorify Your name!" Simple prayer from a son to His Dad.

I got back in the truck and passed another flagpole. The flag was lying limp on the pole. No wind. Smooth ride home.

I thanked Him. I wouldn't have blamed Him if he had not answered that prayer, for I know His judgment is better than mine. He might have had purposes for His wind that were bigger than my comfort. But I was so grateful. Apparently, the way He would be most glorified in that moment was to quell the wind.

INVOLVED

God wants to be engaged in everything in our lives. Big and small. And there are huge residual effects when we pray about everything ... when we pray without ceasing.

Jesus said, "*Up until know you've asked for nothing in my name. Ask, and you will receive, so that your joy may be made full*" (*John 16:24*).

Simple, daily prayer about the small things is more than just a mere request to God. It is one of His ways of training us to turn to Him constantly. To show us the "breadth and length and height and depth" of His love. To know God. To teach us to lean on His breast for matters great and small. To fall in love with Him all over again.

A MODERN-DAY MIRACLE

I know a young man who has been saved from a deeply rebellious life. As He came to Christ, he thought you were supposed to pray about everything. And so, he prays all day long.

He prays for his co-workers at work. He prays about his finances and his relationship to his wife. He prays for random people he meets. He prays about the words that come out of his mouth. He prays about what he puts into his mouth. And, He seeks to listen carefully to the Lord and do precisely as He instructs. Unceasing prayer.

And, guess what? God answers his prayers! All day long. In fact, he bombards me with stories, almost every day of God's answers. The residual of this unceasing prayer is that his days are filled with great joy, such a contrast to his former life! I know this for a fact, for he is one of my sons.

He is continually joyful because he is continually communing with the God who loves him (which would make anyone joyful) and continually receiving answers from the God who provides for him (which brings unceasing joy.)

We have many *joyless* Christians because we have many *prayerless* Christians. You may fall into that camp and, if so, it's time to change—for your sake and His, and for the sake of a watching world. A joyless Christian is an oxymoron and a poor testimony regarding our big God.

It never hurts to ask your Dad.

Pray it in: What prayers have you not asked of God simply because you thought it was insignificant? Ask Him right now! And ask the Lord to help you keep a running dialogue with Him today about *everything*.

DAY 14

A God-sized promise

Some promises seem beyond belief. There are politicians who are masters at unbelievable promises, thinking they can make vows to get elected that they know they cannot fulfill. But they also know that if they offer hope, it secures votes.

The Bible is crowded with 7,000 promises from the God-of-All-Faithfulness. The One who has never failed in all He has promised. In Christ's final conversation with His disciples, He gives a promise so expansive that it is hard to believe. But it is found right before us in the red letters of the inspired, inerrant Scripture.

> *"Truly, truly, I say to you, if you ask the Father for anything in My name, He will give it to you. Until now you have asked for nothing in My name; ask and you will receive, so that your joy may be made full." (John 16:23-24)*

In my name

Fully answered prayer seems too good to be true, but Jesus puts only one limitation on our asking: "In my Name." This restriction is enough, though, to properly align our prayers.

When an Ambassador goes to another nation he carries great power, but it is delegated authority. He has all the resources of his nation at his fingertips. He has access to military might, humanitarian aid, diplomatic resources—the list is endless. But something is very clear: he must represent the will of his authority. He must ask and do only what the nation who sent him desires. He must come fully *in their name*, doing as they would do.

To pray in Christ's name is to carry all His authority and power before the Father, for Jesus said we could come in His name. But, we must listen in prayer to make sure we are praying in accordance with Christ's desires. We must "abide in (Him) and let (His) words abide in us" so that His will becomes ours; His desires, our desires (John 15:7).

Prayers prayed in the Name of Christ are prayers aligned with His will and for His glory. These are prayers initiated by God himself, through the humble, listening believer. And God delights to answer these requests.

ASK AND YOU WILL RECEIVE

God's promise declares that such prayers are *always* answered. Our problem is not that God won't answer, but that we won't stay long enough in the Throne Room to let His heart mold us to His will.

Further, we often won't believe enough to ask boldly. We measure God by our own standards, in humanistic terms. "He couldn't possibly do that," we reason. Because WE can't do something—or we've never seen it done—we assume HE can't do it either. Sadly, we shrink God to our level. As J.B. Phillips wrote, "Your God is too small."

This is precisely what God longs to avoid. He wants to show us that He is God and there is no other. And the way He has designed in this age to accomplish that is through unceasing, God-sized prayers.

FULL JOY

When a believer aligns himself with God, takes Him at His word, and prays these kinds of prayers, God will answer according to His promises. The result for the believer will be a life of great fruitfulness and joy. To any simple believer who prays like this everyday, and sees God answer everyday, their joy will be unending.

God delights to delight His children, just as you do yours. We must give Him that joy by joining Him in unceasing prayer.

Pray it in: What are the areas of your greatest concerns? Begin to ask God today to lead you to a promise from His Word that will give you a faith foundation for your praying.

DAY 15

PRAYING THE PROMISES

IF YOU WERE to have the privilege of reading through my Mother's Bible, you would discover highlighted promises. Beside many of these verses, you would see the various names of each of her children. If you could somehow parallel those verses with the actual life experiences of each of her children, you would discover those promises have been fulfilled in amazing specificity. Mom believed in this process of praying by God's promises, right up to her death. And, it worked with God-glorifying consistency!

A TESTIMONY

Around 1983 my pastor-Dad suffered a terrible moral fall. It rocked our world for several years. At the end of the ordeal, he left my mom, married another woman and moved away. We thought it was the last we would ever see of him.

My mother, before she died two years later, felt she had received a biblical promise from the Lord regarding my Dad. She prayed it often and believed God on his behalf, until the day she died. Here was the promise:

Because he has loved Me, therefore I will deliver him; I
will set him securely on high, because he has known My
name. He will call upon Me, and I will answer him; I
will be with him in trouble; I will rescue him and honor
him. With a long life I will satisfy him and let him see
My salvation. (Psalm 91:14-16)

Five weeks before my mother died, my dad came to a full and complete repentance. Although he had married another and couldn't return to be my Mom's husband, he did return fully to the Lord. His confession was as public as his sin. He stood in the pulpit of almost every church he ever pastored and asked for their forgiveness.

In his remaining years, God greatly used my dad with thousands of pastors. He would humbly warn and instruct them of the subtle work of the enemy to which no man is immune. "No man can rise so high that he cannot fall," he would often say, "and no man can fall so low that he cannot rise again by the grace of God!"

Dad lived 25 years after my mother received and claimed this promise (a "long life"). God honored him in ways which Dad felt he should not be honored. One of those was the forgiveness and love of his family. God used him and "let him see [God's] salvation."

Promise given ... promise believed and prayed ... promise fulfilled.

There are thousands of promises in the Bible, waiting for you. An average of three promises from a faithful God on each page. It seems that this is God's operating system with us. They are given to us to believe and claim in prayer.

What God did for my precious, praying Mom, He will do for you. Read your Bible. Hear His voice. Claim His promises. Pray them in ... and watch God's faithfulness.

Pray it in: Spend a few minutes thanking God for the promises He has already fulfilled in your life. If you have trouble with this, read Ephesians 1:3-14 and give thanks for His faithfulness in your salvation.

DAY 16

THE NECESSITY OF SECLUDED PRAYER

IF A MAN is always available to everyone, he has little left for anyone. Mark, the writer of the second gospel, observed this in the life of Christ.

> *When evening came, after the sun had set, they began bringing to Him all who were ill and those who were demon-possessed. And the whole city had gathered at the door. And He healed many who were ill with various diseases and cast out many demons; and He was not permitting the demons to speak, because they knew who He was.*
>
> ***In the early morning, while it was still dark, Jesus got up, left the house, and went away to a secluded place, and was praying there.*** *Simon and his companions searched for Him; they found Him, and said to Him, "Everyone is looking for You." (Mark 1:32-37, emphasis mine)*

There was an essential pattern in Jesus' life. He was amazingly accessible to people most of the time. During those moments,

He breathed in constant prayer. His Father was telling Him what to say and do right in the middle of intense ministry (John 14:10). This can only occur with unceasing prayer; a practice He would later tell us is essential for fruitful ministry (John 15:1-16; I Thessalonians 5:17).

MORE

But Jesus needed more to sustain maximum effectiveness in ministry. He needed quiet, secluded, personal time with the Father. Since "*all* who were ill and demon-possessed were coming to Him" and "the *whole city* had gathered at the door," Jesus knew that the only way He could have undistracted time with the Father was, "early in the morning, while it was still dark."

"JESUS GOT UP"

It's a simple phrase but telling. "Jesus got up, left the house, and went away to a secluded place."

Most fail right here. When called by God to rise early and make their way to the secluded place, they simply roll over in their beds thinking a few hours' sleep is more valuable than personal communion with the Eternal.

If you study history, you will discover that men and women who were great for God made any sacrifice to spend time alone with Him. It was the treasure hidden in the field, the pearl of great price.

John Hyde, missionary to India, discovered the value of prayer. Work was hard, and people were not coming to Christ. He decided to take more time—often hours—in prayer. Soon, he found that he would walk from a morning in prayer and people would be standing at his door asking, "What do I need to do to be saved?" He discovered that we don't divide prayer from work. Prayer IS the work!

A.J. Gordon said, "You can do more than pray after you've prayed, but you can do nothing but pray until you've prayed."

Those who faithfully pay this price discover this is not merely about getting a few verses for the day or a quick breeze through a laundry list of prayer. God has been waiting for them. He longs for His children to be with Him, knowing certain things are accomplished only in seclusion.

"WENT AWAY TO A SECLUDED PLACE"

Good moms and dads understand this. If they have multiple children, they make time for each one individually. They have things to say to the whole family, but they know personal discipling must happen one-on-one.

Our Father wants to hear and gain the heart of each of His children, which can only be done in private. In these precious moments, a son or daughter can pour out their soul to the One who knows them best. They can be completely transparent with no embarrassment.

Like King David, they can lament and doubt, question and cry as they discharge their hearts to God. But before the secluded time is over, they will hear the Father speak the exact words they need. They will feel His everlasting arms beneath them and around them, comforting and encouraging. They will know they are enveloped in unconditional love. He will give the words necessary to bring them back to faith and rest. Read the Psalms and you will see this pattern repeated continually in David's prayers.

"AND WAS PRAYING THERE"

Can this be said of you? Do you rise with eagerness at the prompting of the Spirit? Do you enter expectantly into the Holy of Holies, humbled by the privilege of spending time in the glorious presence of the God-Who-Sees? Do you meet Him there? Do you wait on Him to hear what He wants to say to you in private? Do you listen to His Word through the Scriptures? Do you exchange words of affection? And do you leave that place equipped to give a fresh word to those He will bring across your path that day?

If this is your practice, you will have everything you need for everyone. You will not give people the noxious fumes of an exhausted life. The fragrance of heaven will be upon you—a fragrance that entices them to enter the secluded place themselves.

Pray it in: Ask God to awaken you every morning this week—at a time of His choosing—for prayer and the study of His Word. When you wake up, get up! There are other times for sleep, but nothing more valuable than time with Him.

DO YOU HEAR HIM?

EVERY PLACE IN this world God created is proclaiming God, but most do not recognize it as such. And most do not—upon hearing His voice—give Him the glory He deserves. Men call the world around them "nature." The Bible calls it "God's Voice."

DAVID HEARD THE VOICE

Seven times in Psalm, Chapter 29, David speaks of the "voice of the Lord" speaking through the mighty things he sees and hears happening around him. David heard God's voice in the thunder, lightning, earthquake, and storms.

He heard God's voice in the temple where everything around him was shouting, "Glory!" He heard and saw God as he realized his King was sovereign over everything. Creation showed him that "the Lord sits as King forever."

He saw God as the One who was "giving strength to His people" and blessing His people with the gift of peace. He recognized the Source behind what He was experiencing personally and what His people were experiencing.

THE PROPER RESPONSE

... is seen in the opening lines of this Psalm.

> *Ascribe to the Lord, O sons of the mighty, ascribe to the Lord glory and strength. Ascribe to the Lord the glory due to His name; worship the Lord in holy array. (Psalm 29:1-2)*

To "ascribe" means to acknowledge who is the rightful Creator and Author of these things. We are to so understand the voice of God in nature that we realize He is the cause behind it all.

And there is but one response: "Worship the Lord in the majesty of holiness." We are to let His voice draw us to bent knees, lifted hands, raised voices, surrendered lives in true worship. And, if we are hearing Him all day, we will be worshiping Him every hour!

THE COMBINATION

A great man I know has adopted the regular practice of taking his Bible, a lawn chair, and a bottle of water into nature. He enjoys everything he sees along the way, and then he sits in a beautiful spot in God's creation and reads whole books of the Bible God wrote.

You may think you could not have this luxury, but this man is a very busy and highly regarded medical doctor—probably far busier than you. But he makes a conscious, intentional choice, and his testimony is that this regular practice centers his life.

He will tell you that the combination of the Word of God, and the Spirit of God, in the Creation of God magnifies God's voice exponentially. It never ceases to correct his perspective, calm his soul, renew his mind, tenderize his will. This triple-antidote works on his wounded soul and brings healing.

But the greatest result of this exercise? Worship. In such times, he cannot help but burst into praise. It is my suspicion that this doctor is not the only one who is pleased.

Pray it in: Get your calendar out and plan a day or a half-day for time away with God. Don't make excuses. Consider fasting on this day. Take a notebook and record what God is saying to you. There is nothing more valuable than time with Him!

DAY 18

FACING THE PLACE OF SURRENDER IN PRAYER

DO A QUICK scan of the Scripture and you will notice that men and women were placed on purpose by God in various environments. Adam and Eve in the Garden, Abraham in Canaan, Moses in the bulrushes—God put people where He desired to accomplish things that could have happened nowhere else. And, He does the same with each of us.

Often we don't see our geography as such and we resist and run from these places. But we must be wise to God's greater agenda. If we are to experience all God has, we must embrace each environment, even if it's hard.

THE PLACE OF DISTRESS

> *Then Jesus came with them to a **place called Gethsemane**, and said to His disciples, "Sit here while I go over there and pray." And He took with Him Peter and the two sons of Zebedee and began to be grieved and distressed.*
>
> *Then He said to them, "My soul is deeply grieved, to the point of death; remain here and keep watch with*

Me." And He went a little beyond them, and fell on His
face and prayed, saying, "My Father, if it is possible, let
this cup pass from Me, yet not as I will, but as You will."
(Matthew 26:36-39, emphasis mine)

Jesus knew what lay ahead. The deepest suffering any human would ever experience was His to drink. The man, Jesus, looked at this cup with dread. He "fell on His face" in prayer. Another gospel writer says that before this time of wrestling was over, His sweat became like great drops of blood.

Although He could have, God did not deliver His Son from this place. The Father could have swept in and rescued Jesus from this painful night of prayer and the events that were to follow. But for Divine, world-changing reasons, this cup was Christ's to drink.

There are times when God knows we must go through such wrestling as we face the possibilities of following God. These times are not random, but deliberate, just as it was with Jesus.

A PLACE OF DEEP SURRENDER

It is easy to speak of surrender sitting in a nice chair in an air-conditioned auditorium. These are not unmeaningful times and often are incredibly legitimate. But look at Jesus. He knew—with full realization—what was before Him. He faced the suffering with reality. And, He found that reality in a place of prayer.

He also knew that this path would bring glory to the Father and deliverance to those He had come to save. In the greatest act of surrender ever experienced by mortal man, Jesus cried out, "Not my will but Thine be done."

Deep distress is often the pathway to deep surrender. God hears our distress and will meet us where we are, but He does not always deliver us from the suffering. This life is brief, and He has purposeful places for us beyond our understanding. They are most often pathways that open the gate to bring salvation and life to others.

THE RESPONSE

So, what should we do when we find ourselves in such a place? We should "fall on [our face] and pray" as He did. We should face the reality squarely, without silliness or false hopes. We should take others with us to pray (even if they may fall asleep, not knowing the depth of what we are experiencing). And, if we are to be used as our Firstborn Brother was used to glorify God, we must come to the blessed place of full surrender to God's will.

But we must also know that, at the end of suffering, there is joy! Jesus was the One, "who for the joy set before Him endured the cross, despising the shame, and has sat down at the right hand of God" (Hebrews 12:2). The will of God is always best for all concerned, even though the path to its acceptance may be painful.

Joy comes in the morning! We must remember this, and gladly go to this sacred place in prayer.

Pray it in: What step of surrender are you facing right now? Take time to pray through this. If you find yourself unwilling to let go, ask God to make you willing ... and then release it into His hands.

DAY 19

OUR SACRED PRIVILEGE
AND SERIOUS RESPONSIBILITY

Aaron shall carry the names of the sons of Israel in the breastpiece
of judgment over his heart when he enters the holy place, for a
memorial before the Lord continually.

(EXODUS 28:29)

AARON WAS THE high priest and, as such, had a very serious task.
He was to enter into the presence of the Lord and represent the
people before God. This is why he carried the people's names on
his breastpiece, right over his heart. Once in the Holy of Holies,
intercession would be made for the people's sins so they would
be forgiven. This spiritual transaction happened at the "mercy
seat."

All of this, of course, was a symbol and picture of Christ and
what he would do in the coming days. Christ, our High Priest,
would enter in and give His blood for our pardon. He carried our
names on His heart as He entered there on Calvary—a sacrifice
which would buy our eternal pardon.

Your name was there. Right over his heart.

OUR INTERCESSION

We are not exactly like Christ in His unique role except in this way: we are now "Kings and Priests" and our main responsibility is to bring people to God. We are to intercede on behalf of others and also tell them the good news of what Christ has done for them. We are His ambassadors as "though God were entreating through us" to reconcile people to God (2 Corinthians 5:20).

In prayer now, we can walk each day into the Throne room and intercede for people. Notice the parallels:

- We must carry people's names on our hearts;

- We must enter the holy place on their behalf;

- We must come before the Lord, (who is a faithful God who hears and answers); and,

- We must do this continually.

OUR NAMES

Over the course of our lives, we will encounter thousands of people. They are grazing across our lives on purpose. These are lives—names—of those we are to bring before God!

Are their personal names on our hearts? No one else may take up that responsibility. Are we entering the throne room on their behalf? And, will we do it until we die, or they come to Christ?

George Mueller carried a burden for the salvation of two childhood friends until his death. He believed that God had placed them there and they would be saved as a result of prayer offered to a prayer hearing and prayer answering God.

One of the men was saved at Mueller's funeral. The other came to Christ six months after his death.

Pray it in: What names has God placed on your heart and what does God want for each of them individually? Would you ask God what He desires for them specifically, and spend time bringing them before Him right now in prayer?

DAY 20

THE ONLY PLACE WE CAN MEET GOD

You shall put the mercy seat on top of the ark and in the ark, you shall put the testimony which I will give to you. There I will meet with you; and from above the mercy seat, from between the cherubim which are upon the ark of the testimony, I will speak to you about all that I will give you in commandment for the sons of Israel.

(EXODUS 25:21-22)

WHEN GOD LED his people out of Egypt's bondage, He initiated the building of a tabernacle. He wanted there to be a recognizable place that would speak of the sacrifice of His coming Son. A place of holiness. A place of mercy. Every single thing about this tabernacle was by His design, and each part had perfect meaning and purpose.

In the holiest, inner portion of this tabernacle was the Ark of the Covenant, the most sacred piece of furniture built. And, on top of the Ark was what God designated as the "mercy seat." Literally the word means the "propitiary or atonement seat." Big word. Bigger meaning.

GRACIOUS MERCY

"Atonement" means to "cover over, propitiate, pacify." It means that the sins which were once seen and created our guilt are now covered by God.

It is fascinating and instructive that this was the place where God said, "There I will meet with you." God is everywhere, but in the legal sense for God and His people, this is the only place where we can encounter Him ... at the place of His mercy. There our sins are covered. There we are clean before Him.

Because of Christ, the veil was torn that separated us from the Holy of Holies and now we can enter and experience the presence of Christ all the time. Our sins are covered by His sacrifice. But, we must remember the price that was paid to bring us this gift.

NEVER FORGET

We may take meeting with God in prayer as a nice, occasional opportunity, and treat it lightly. If we're not thoughtful, we can waltz in and out of His presence with little thought of what has happened to allow us to enter this holiest place.

But we should stop and remember.

Remember the false accusations Christ endured from the very people He created. The scorn and ridicule. Pause and think of the metal-tipped, leather whips that ripped the flesh from His body, making Him unrecognizable. Ponder His walk toward Golgotha as people cried out around Him in anger.

And then walk with Him to the cross. Hear the nails ripping human flesh. The dull thud of the cross into the hole prepared. Watch His body as it is contorted into a posture that brought slow and certain death.

Remember that "He who knew no sin" was becoming sin on our behalf (2 Corinthians 5:21). Observe in silence the moment of greatest grief as the Father looked upon His Son—the One with whom He had enjoyed perfect fellowship for eternity—and poured the full weight of His wrath upon the sin-laden Christ. Observe Jesus bearing this grueling punishment of separation from the Father. Watch Him enduring hell for our sin.

And as He cried with His last breath, "It is finished!" watch the massive veil of the temple torn from top to bottom. The veil that separated us from the mercy seat. And realize it was torn by none other than God, inviting us all to enter into His presence freely because of the sacrifice of His Son.

Remember these moments as you approach Him in prayer and come in humble gratitude. It cost Christ His life for this curtain to be torn and the way made for you to enter God's presence. For us to be able to enjoy the privilege of prayer.

Do not treat this lightly or handle it with little respect or casual commitment. It is an amazing act of His mercy that it is available at all.

Pray it in: Spend time in prayer making no request, but simply thanking Christ for all He did to allow you to enter His presence in prayer.

DAY 21

WHY WE MUST UNITE
IN PRAYER

*These all with one mind were continually
devoting themselves to prayer.*

(ACTS 1:14)

ASK ANYONE WHO knows you well and they will easily be able to
tell about your ways. "Well, he/she always does (this)." "If you
approach him/her this way, it will be better because ..." There are
certain things about how you function—your operating systems.

Just as you have your ways, God has His, and they are recognizable. He has designed the necessary means for us to access His
life and power. The Word of God, preaching, worship, communion, etc. are all in this category. They are beautifully catalogued
for us in the closing verses of Acts, Chapter Two.

We didn't invent these, but we can cooperate with God in
humility, using His means. And, if we do, He will graciously
respond by giving us, and those with us, more than we can think
or imagine.

THE FOUNDATIONAL MEANS

... of engaging God is "Spirit-led, Scripture-fed prayer," as Daniel Henderson says. We often view prayer as a side-room, but it is the foundation. We have no real relationship with God unless we pray. (How would a marriage be described if a husband and wife never talked with each other, communicating needs, hurts, desires, and daily decisions?)

Our life begins with prayer and is developed and sustained by prayer. Paul reminds us that, "Whoever *calls* on the name of the Lord will be saved" (Romans 10:13, emphasis mine).

If Christ is the Head of the church, how can we possibly say that we are a church if we do not let Him speak to us and spend large amounts of time communing with Him?

The early church understood this. In Acts 1:14, you find them doing exactly what Christ told them to do which would bring about all the results for which they longed. They were learning, just as they had seen for three years as they walked with Jesus, that the primary means of advancing the Kingdom was to commune with the Father. Notice each phrase:

- "**These all**" (No one was absent, for this was the highest priority.)

- "**with one mind**" (Prayer led them to unity. In prayer, selfish ideas were melted away and God's ideas became important for everyone.)

- "**were continually**" (There was no thought of anything else—it was their habitual practice.)

- "**devoting themselves**" (To be devoted means to "be strong towards" and they were, individually, making the choice to pray together.)

- "**to prayer**" (The primary, foundational means of getting God's work done.)

UNITED PRAYER

For 25 years, in the town where I have pastored, we have attempted to do the same. We have sought to come together, continually, with one mind to pray—first as pastors in the city and then to gather our people together in prayer. Each year that this happens, the kingdom advances.

Only heaven will record the results, but when we cooperate together in prayer, there is always an increase in unity, connection, and direction from God about our city. And spiritual momentum occurs.

The sad reality of our fragmented, self-focused, ambitious church life in most cities, is that many don't view this means of grace as foundational. But those of us who have engaged in united prayer have experienced it and believe.

What if this happened in your city? With all the churches who name the name of Christ? Before you brush aside the idea, read the rest of Acts, Chapters 1 and 2, and see the explosion of God's grace.

There is more at stake than any of us realize. United prayer is uniquely irresistible to God. Our cities need the spiritual awakening that could occur when all the people "with one mind are continually devoting themselves to prayer."

Pray it in: Find someone to pray with this week. Also, when your pastors invite you to pray with others—in your church or your city—recognize the value of united prayer and eagerly join in.

DAY 22

FINDING GOD IN THE MIDST OF YOUR TROUBLE

EVERY DAY, IF we are wise, we will realize our increasing need for God. We were designed to depend on Him, just like our lungs crave oxygen and our heart needs blood.

This world is full of difficulties that are beyond us. Of problems that at any moment threaten to pull us down into the quicksand of despair and defeat. Of decisions that are above our capabilities. We need Someone bigger.

So, how do we find Him in the midst of such a troubled and fallen world?

THE HONEST QUESTION

> *"How long will You forget me, O Lord? How long will You hide Your face from me? How long must I lay up cares within me and have sorrow in my heart day after day? How long shall my enemy exalt himself over me?"* (Psalm 13:1-2, Amplified Bible)

David is describing in prayer what life feels like at the moment.

It seems like the Lord has forsaken Him. He doesn't sense His presence. He is overcome with cares and sorrow. His enemies seem to be winning the day.

Every person has days like this. David's Psalm strikes a chord in us because of his raw, unfiltered honesty. He's voicing what is in our hearts when it seems God is distant and unconcerned.

THE FERVENT PRAYER

> "Consider and answer me, O Lord my God; lighten the eyes (of my faith to behold Your face in the pitch-like darkness), lest I sleep the sleep of death, lest my enemy say, 'I have prevailed over him,' and those that trouble me rejoice when I am shaken." (Psalm 13:3-4, Amplified Bible)

David does the one thing that a fallen, helpless man in a fallen, helpless world can do: He cries out. In fervent prayer, He asks God to answer him and enlighten his eyes to see the real truth and the bigger picture.

This is what we need. An ant looks at a large stone in front of him and sees it as an insurmountable obstacle. We look at the scene and see a clear path for the ant if he will simply walk around the rock to the food on the other side. It is a mountain to an ant, but a molehill to a human. It is huge to the small, but inconsequential to the one who is above.

God is above our trouble. He sees it with Divine perspective. David asks God for the eyes of faith to see with God's clarity so he will not be overwhelmed with despair.

THE REDEEMING FAITH

> *"But I have trusted, leaned on, and been confident in Your*
> *mercy and loving-kindness; my heart shall rejoice and be*
> *in high spirits in Your salvation. I will sing to the Lord,*
> *because He has dealt bountifully with me." (Psalm 13:5-6,*
> *Amplified Bible)*

At the end of his prayer, David is reminded of the lovingkindness of God. Think of that word. God is not only loving towards us, but also kind. Everything He does is driven by this never-changing attribute.

David remembers that God is a Savior in the full sense of that word. He has saved him over and over from trouble and He will not forsake him now. The Lord speaks to David, because he prayed. He comes to the place of being in "high spirits," and even singing to the Lord! He knows—in spite of all the seemingly overwhelming problems around him—that God will deal bountifully with him.

Are you in this David moment? There is one remedy, and only one. Come to the Father with honest questions and a fervent cry. It will lead you to a refueled faith and a rejoicing heart.

Pray it in: Pray through the specific issues you are facing right now. "Cast all your care upon God, because He cares for you" (1 Peter 5:7).

DAY 23

7 QUESTIONS THE ENEMY
IS ALWAYS ASKING YOU

(OR, HOW HE TAKES YOU OUT
BEFORE THE BATTLE BEGINS)

WE ARE OFTEN unaware, and our ignorance is our downfall. Satan, our powerful, constant enemy, is "prowling about like a lion, seeking whom he may devour." Some of his primary schemes against us are relentless question-asking, doubt-raising, and accusing.

If we are clueless about the diabolical source of these questions, we will see them as merely our own thoughts. We will pay little attention to their genesis and naively let them lodge in our souls, debilitating and defeating us.

SEVEN QUESTIONS
King Hezekiah was surrounded by the army of Sennacherib, the king of Assyria, who had come to besiege Jerusalem and destroy God's people. Part of Sennacherib's strategy from the beginning, no doubt led by the Great Enemy himself, was to send his servants to ask questions and raise doubts in the minds of

the people (2 Chronicles 32). This was purely designed to create fear and win the battle of the mind. If he could intimidate the people, he would be victorious without lifting a spear.

You will notice this tactic used throughout the Bible, including Satan's attacks on Eve in the Garden and Jesus in the wilderness. He is not very original with this scheme—he doesn't need to be.

Look at these questions carefully because Satan has not changed them much. The questions are modernized for each generation, but at the base they are the same fiery darts of the Wicked One. If you stop, you will realize these have been posed to your thinking hundreds of times. Pause and read through 2 Chronicles, Chapter 32, and notice the Enemy's constant assaults on your faith, as seen below.

1. **Is God really trustworthy?**
   "Thus says Sennacherib king of Assyria, 'On what are you trusting that you are remaining in Jerusalem under siege?'" (Vs. 10)

2. **Isn't God lying to you?**
   "Is not Hezekiah misleading you to give yourselves over to die by hunger and by thirst, saying, 'The Lord our God will deliver us from the hand of the king of Assyria?'" (Vs. 11)

3. **Is God's plan reliable? Isn't it foolish? Illogical? Unreasonable?**
   "Has not the same Hezekiah taken away His high places and His altars, and said to Judah and Jerusalem, 'You shall

worship before one altar, and on it you shall burn incense?'"
(Vs. 12)

4. **Do you know how impossible this problem is? You might as well go ahead and give up!**

   "Do you not know what I and my fathers have done to all the peoples of the lands?" (Vs. 13)

5. **Hasn't God failed you in the past? Remember that time you (or others) trusted Him and it didn't work?**

   "Were the gods of the nations of the lands able at all to deliver their land from my hand?" (Vs. 13)

6. **Do you think you're better than others who've faced this? This issue has defeated stronger people than you.**

   "Who was there among all the gods of those nations which my fathers utterly destroyed who could deliver his people out of my hand, that your God should be able to deliver you from my hand?" (Vs. 14)

7. **You know that God can't deliver you, right?**

   "Now therefore, do not let Hezekiah deceive you or mislead you like this, and do not believe him, for no god of any nation or kingdom was able to deliver his people from my hand or from the hand of my fathers. How much less will your God deliver you from my hand?" (Vs. 15)

A GODLY DEFENSE

So, how do you overcome this unceasing onslaught? It must be met with unceasing prayer! Notice Hezekiah's response to these fiery darts of doubt.

> But King Hezekiah and Isaiah the prophet, the son of Amoz, **prayed about this and cried out to heaven**. And the Lord sent an angel who destroyed every mighty warrior, commander and officer in the camp of the king of Assyria. So, he returned in shame to his own land. (Vs. 20-21, emphasis mine)

Hezekiah, and his friend in ministry, Isaiah, went to God in prayer and cried out for deliverance. Apparently, God was just waiting for someone to ask him. He was quick to defend His sons and bring judgment upon the enemy. God hates bullies who try to demoralize His people, and He will exalt His children who turn to Him in humble, persevering faith.

If Hezekiah and Isaiah had not prayed, would these demonic questions have lodged in their minds? Deterred them from their work? Allowed the enemies of God to win the day?

Most assuredly. But that's not how the story ended for them, and not how it has to end for you ... if you will pray.

Pray it in: Spend time in prayer asking God what lies from the Enemy you have believed. Resist the Enemy, firm in your faith and renounce each lie. Then, pray the TRUTH in about each area.

DAY 24

A DAILY PRAYER IN THE MIDST
OF A BRIEF LIFE!

WE THINK WE will last forever. This is why we can waste hours, that turn into days, that turn into years. "Someday" soon, we'll make the right choices and live for what matters. But the Psalmist, in Psalm 90, recognized the brevity of life.

> *As for the days of our life, they contain seventy years, or if due to strength, eighty years ... for soon it is gone and we fly away. (Psalm 90:10)*

We act as if there are many days to accomplish the work set before us, when in reality there are but few. It is vitally important that each day be maximized. The surest path to their usefulness is a life of unceasing prayer so that God is acknowledged and depended upon every moment of every day.

Notice the four things the Psalmist prayed for—a great daily prayer for us!

1. **For wisdom to remember the brevity of life**.

   "So, teach us to number our days that we may present to You

a heart of wisdom." (Vs. 12)

2. **For God's lovingkindness in the morning, so we can know gladness and joy every single day**.
   "O satisfy us in the morning with Your lovingkindness that we may sing for joy and be glad all our days." (Vs. 14)
   That our souls would be satisfied with God (which would keep us from chasing other gods!)

3. **For the ability to see God's work, and a vision of God's majesty to fill the minds and hearts of our children**.
   "Let Your work appear to Your servants and Your majesty to their children." (Vs. 16)
   So that we can leave a legacy that will last beyond us—a legacy built through prayer.

4. **For God's favor, for all of life is nothing without His grace!**
   "Let the favor of the Lord our God be upon us; and confirm for us the work of our hands!" (Vs. 17)
   His favor is what will make our work established and meaningful and blessed. "Confirm" means to "give permanence to." Therefore, the Psalmist is praying that the work he does will be established by God in such ways that it will last beyond his life.

Pray it in: Thoughtfully pray this prayer this morning ...

Precious Father, help me to realize today that my life is brief and let me deal with every moment with wisdom. Satisfy my heart this morning with the fullness of Your lovingkindness. Help me understand and experience that you are not only loving, but You are also kind. Fill me with such joy that I will sing before others. Let my heart be so satisfied in You that I will not go in silent search for other lovers.

Help me to see Your work all around me today. Open my mind to see You in everything. Give my children the eyes to see Your majesty surrounding them so they will increasingly worship You.

And Lord, place Your favor and grace upon us all today. So work in and through us that we will build that which You initiate and may it last beyond us for Your glory!

DAY 25

A CLEAR AND PRESENT DANGER

SLEEP IS THE most natural response in the world. When you are tired from long work or stressful activities, there is a God-built tendency to close your eyes and drift into rest. There's nothing wrong with this, unless you are in a situation where watchfulness is critical.

For instance, if you are in the military and the sole watchmen on the front lines, you cannot sleep. To err here not only endangers your life, but the lives of all those you protect.

There are moments for followers of Christ where spiritual sleep is deadly. When the great Enemy of our souls is on the prowl, to drift into spiritual repose is exactly what he desires.

A LESSON ON SLEEP

Jesus had just warned His disciples at the last supper that a time of temptation was coming. He told them in advance that they would all run away and he would be killed. Grieved with the impending suffering He was to endure, He took his three, most trusted men with Him to His common place of prayer and asked them to stay awake and be watchful.

When He returned from private prayer, He found them sound

asleep. Always teaching, Jesus uses the moment to give a critical lesson.

> *"So you men could not keep watch with Me for one hour? Keep watching and praying that you may not enter into temptation; the spirit is willing, but the flesh is weak." (Matthew 26:41)*

Kenneth Wuest in his wonderful "Expanded Translation of the New Testament" helps us see this verse more clearly:

> *Be ever watching and be ever praying lest you enter a place of testing where a solicitation to do evil may be the occasion which will lead to an act of sin." (Matthew 26:40-41)*

BE EVER WATCHING

Jesus knew the enemy was coming. He had warned his men. But even with this immediate warning, His disciples failed to keep watch.

Satan and his minions are always on the prowl. If we are to avoid his temptations, we must keep our spiritual eyes open. And, there are some moments when we are more vulnerable and the danger more present than others.

In this day in our nation, when the walls are down and the enemy has increased leverage, this is even more important.

BE EVER PRAYING

Seasons of Satan's strong attacks must be combatted in unceasing prayer. There is only One who can help us see temptation for what it really is and give us grace to be victorious. Only One who can alert us to the presence of the evil One and identify his whispers for what they really are. Only One who can look behind enemy lines and alert us when deadly missiles are poised and about to be fired upon us, our families, or our church. Therefore, the lines of communication must be open always to the Father in prayer. It must be the air we breathe.

OUR WEAKNESS

... is our flesh, Jesus said. Our redeemed spirits—regenerated by the Spirit of God within us—may long to stay awake and watchful. But our humanity is weak during this present age. It will pull us to slumber if we are not careful.

Prayer is not merely a "nice thing" to do to get a few things you need. It is your protection and lifeline from all that is threatening your soul and the lives of those you are charged to protect. You would never fall asleep if you knew a mortal enemy was prowling about your house, intent on killing your children.

Paul, realizing this, tell us in Ephesians, Chapter 6, to put on the full armor of God and then do one thing: "With **all** prayer and petition pray at **all** times in the Spirit, and with this in view, be on the alert with **all** perseverance and petition for **all** the saints" (Ephesians 6:18, *emphasis mine*)

It's time to wake up, and stay awake, in prayer.

Pray it in: Turn to Ephesians 6:10-20. Pray through this armor, asking God to cover your life and keep you alert in prayer.

DAY 26

HOW DO I HANDLE THE TRIALS OF MY LIFE RIGHT NOW?

IN COLLEGE, MY future wife, Holly, and I decided to memorize James, Chapter 1, together. We had no idea how we would revisit these powerful promises the rest of our lives!

As I write these words, I'm up early this morning wrestling through a trial and burden once again. I cried out, while praying in bed before I got up, *"Lord, what should I do?"*

As I rose to begin my normal, systematic reading through God's Word, I came to this familiar passage. For the first time, I saw James 1:2-6 as five very practical, clear COMMANDS, accompanied by incredible PROMISES. And, these words became an intimate message this morning from my Father to me once again. They are not just to be read, but believed and prayed.

Here is what I am to do ... and what God says He will do. Perhaps you're facing some trials and need to pray these specific prayers along with me today.

1. **Consider it all joy, when you encounter various trials** (James 1:2)

    Obviously, this is the exact opposite of my normal response.

I consider it all anguish, or consider it all a burden, or consider it something I want to get rid of or solve quickly and go on to life. But this IS life.

> *"Lord, I choose, this morning, to rejoice. I take all the aspects of my trial and lay them before You. You knew about this a million years ago and have everything I need for 'life and godliness.' I can trust You. I choose to consider this 'all joy.' Not some joy. Not a lot of grief, but a little joy. But, ALL joy!*
>
> *"By Your grace, I will not let what my human eyes see in the physical world determine what I believe, because there is another world—a spiritual, heavenly realm where reality is complete. I believe that, as you have decreed from that heavenly realm, you are working this together for good. I choose **joy** this morning."*

The reason for this admonition is stated in the next verse.

2. **Knowing that the testing of your faith produces endurance** (Vs. 2)

I am admonished by God to remember that my trials have a great purpose, both in me and others. It is the "testing of my faith" and is sent or allowed to "produce endurance."

Endurance is faith stretched out. It is faith that has been so tested that it is able to go to the finish line. It is the faith that I will need to meet future task and trials. Without this test, I will be ill equipped to face the next challenges. God knows this and is preparing me. Endurance will give me the calmness that is able to entrust any burden to God. And, the greatest evidence of that faith is joy!

> *"Lord, thank You for this reminder. Thank You that You have a purpose in this for me and all concerned. You are building me because You love me. You are willing to let me not understand the details so I can learn to trust the details to you. So, Lord, right now, I choose to remember what you're doing."*

3. **And let endurance have its perfect result** (Vs. 4)

   I must be willing to let this trial run its full course. It is there to produce something, so I must let it do its full work.

   As I let this trial accomplish its purposes, it will make me "perfect and complete, lacking in nothing." In other words, it will build my faith in ways that nothing else can. This trial (the one I'm facing RIGHT NOW) falls in that category. I must cooperate with God in all He is telling me to do, learning all He longs for me to learn, and rejoicing that there are such purposes from a sovereign God.

   > *"Lord, as painful as this seems to me, You will not test me beyond the limits You have set for my life. So, gracious Father, take it all the way. I know You will give me sufficient grace, but I tell You this morning that I desire for this trial to have its full effect—to do its full work in me and those who are involved. I embrace Your sovereignty, Lord. You have never failed me, and You never will."*

4. **But if any of you lack wisdom, let him ask God** (Vs. 5)
Here is a further command. "Do you not know what to
do? Then here is your path: cry out to God! Ask Him for
direction. And here is a promise: He is a God who gives
wisdom to "all generously and without reproach." If you
ask Him it "will be given" to you, and He won't make fun
of you for asking!

So, this morning, I'm asking.

> *"Lord, give me wisdom. I don't have a clue what
> to do in this situation. I've never been here. So,
> give me wisdom that is far beyond my own human
> understanding."*

5. **But he must ask in faith without any doubting** (Vs. 6)
James reminds us that the man who asks without faith is
like a wave that is tossed back and forth by the wind and
he will receive nothing from the Lord.

> *"Lord, I'm coming in faith. I believe you have
> purpose in this trial. I believe you will hold true to
> your promise because you are the God who cannot
> lie. I believe that you will give me the wisdom I
> need. I will rejoice, I will endure by faith. I will
> trust You, and I will keep trusting You, by Your
> grace!"*

Pray it in: Walk back through this chapter and pray each of
these prayers for areas of need in your own life or the life of
someone you know who needs wisdom.

DAY 27

8 POWERFUL PRAYERS TO PRAY FOR THOSE YOU LOVE!

PAUL'S PRAYERS ARE given to inspire us, but also to teach us how to pray. Like the Lord's Prayer, they are beautiful, but also instructive.

We have much to learn from his prayer in Colossians 1:9-12. First, we should learn from the persistence of his prayers, as Paul said he "did not cease" to pray for them. We must pray without ceasing.

For instance, what if we would choose, like Paul, to intercede unceasingly for our children? Or for fellow church members? Or our pastor? Or, for people far from God? What if we spent our life praying this simple, powerful, life-changing prayer that Paul prayed, for everyone we know?

We are never on more solid ground than when we pray exactly what is contained in the God-breathed words of Scripture. Right now, before you read further, walk through this prayer for someone God has placed in your path. Pray that they will be...

1. **Filled with the knowledge of God's will in all spiritual wisdom and understanding** (Vs. 9)

2. **So they will walk in a manner worthy of the Lord** (Vs. 10)

3. **To please Him in all respects** (Vs. 10)

4. **Bearing fruit in every good work** (Vs. 10)

5. **And increasing in the knowledge of God** (Vs. 10)

6. **Strengthened with all power, according to God's glorious might** (Vs. 11)

7. **Attaining all steadfastness and patience** (Vs. 11)

8. **Joyously giving thanks to the Father, who has qualified us to share in the inheritance of the saints in the Light** (Vs. 12)

Now, pray it through again, thinking more deeply and adding deliberate details that God brings across your mind with each segment of the prayer.

If you did nothing more, the rest of your life, than pray this simple prayer for those God places in your life, you will have accomplished more than most for the Kingdom. And you will find them thanking you in heaven for the faithfulness of your intercession on their behalf and the fruit it has borne.

And you will hear God say, "Well, done!"

Pray it in: Seek to memorize this simple, powerful prayer as a ready tool in your prayer life. Write down this prayer passage in your journal and pray it daily over your family.

DAY 28

WHAT DO YOU DO IN THE PIT?

Out of the depths I have cried to You Lord. O Lord, hear my voice!

(PSALM 130:1-2)

WE ALL FIND ourselves there, some more frequently than others. Something has happened to take us to the depths of despair, or sin, or confusion, or depression ... or whatever.

There's a reason the Psalmist in Psalm 130 calls it "the depths." This is no surface malady—it goes deeper. It's something you can't get rid of yourself. It's a place of helplessness and hopelessness. It's a valley of deep pain and sorrow. It may be something you brought on yourself by your own sin or foolishness, or it was created by others. But nonetheless, you're there ... and it's painful.

Not only can this affect an individual, it can be the summary condition of an entire nation. A nation that has run from God and is under God's judgment. A nation that has lost its way. A nation in the depths.

So, what do you do?

CRY OUT

"Out of the depths I have cried to You, O Lord." (Vs. 1)

If you physically fell into a deep, inescapable pit, you would cry out for any chance passerby. It would be a desperate cry. You would know that no one may hear, but if someone did, they alone would be your salvation.

The Psalmist's prayer is no random cry. This is directed to the only One who can save him. The One who hears and answers. The One who can lift nations with the motion of His hand. The One who has all power and the One who is driven by abundant mercy and overwhelming grace. This is a cry to the Sovereign God of the Universe.

Crying out is always a sign of desperation. It is what we do when everything else has failed and there is no place else to turn.

If we are in the depths, we must cry out to the Lord. I have, through the years, found myself simply crying, "Help!" to the Lord in my deepest pits. He hears that cry.

CONFIDENTLY WAIT ON HIS WORD

"I wait for the Lord, my soul does wait, and in His word do I hope." (Vs. 5)

When we are in a pit, we need a word from God. We need to go to His Scripture (which is given for this purpose) and ask Him to give us specific instructions and promises. The Bible is a personal book, designed in a supernatural way to be the living and active words from Christ to us in every Word and every way needed. It is these words that ignite faith.

And then we must wait. The most aggressive thing you can do in a pit is to seek Him and wait on Him. Waiting is not passive, but the active dependency and expectancy towards a faithful God.

Where I am seated, as I write this, is in a dining room in a hotel that is tended by a very good waiter. He is regularly coming to me, checking on me, asking me for any instructions I would have for him. This is to be our posture as we wait on God. We must keep our eyes tuned to Christ as we are in the pit. He will give us everything we need while waiting and relying on His Word.

And as we cry out and wait on the Lord, what are the results?

FORGIVENESS

"If you, O, Lord should mark iniquities, O Lord, who could stand? But there is forgiveness with You, that You may be feared." (Vss. 3-4)

It is the most amazing part of God because it is so foreign to our natural way of thinking. He forgives. Whenever He hears a truly humble, repentant cry, He releases the debt and removes the load from our shoulders. He is "faithful and just to forgive us our sins and cleanse us from all unrighteousness" (1 John 1:9). As quickly as you repent, He is quick to forgive.

If you are in the pit because of your sin, or have deepened the pit through your sin, why would you continue to stay there? Quit rationalizing, blaming, and manipulating, and cry out for His cleansing.

LOVINGKINDNESS

"For with the Lord there is lovingkindness." (Vs. 7)

We would expect different because we are different. But

when we cry from the pit, looking to Him, we will discover He is purely and eternally kind. He is perfect in His judgments—powerful when men rebel against Him—but behind it all is perfect love and kindness. It is eternally so with God.

Why would you not cry out to the One who is perfect in lovingkindness?

ABUNDANT REDEMPTION

"And with Him is abundant redemption." (Vs. 7)

No one else can do this. No one can pull us out of these pits but God. He does it effortlessly. He can lift whole nations by a move of His hand and bring revival and spiritual awakening. Why would we think He could not abundantly deliver us?

Do not put timetables or requirements upon Him. He is never in a hurry but always on time. If His deliverance is not to our liking, then we must check our heart. His timing is always related to our good, other's salvation, and His glory.

Are you in a pit? You have multiple choices. You can manipulate, scheme, and work to seek alternate routes, but it will not deliver you. You can wallow in self-pity, all the while blaming everyone else for your terrible condition, even blaming God. You can rationalize that others are in similar pits and you will simply join them in destruction. You can seek temporary pleasure and relief to ease your pain, but when you wake up from your stupor you will discover that you have merely dug the hole deeper.

Or, you can pray. Humbly, repentantly, confidently looking to the Savior. And the best time to cry out is *now*.

Pray it in: Are you in a pit today? Perhaps you need to bring your burden to God and let His lovingkindness wash over you in prayer. Take a moment, with open hands, and admit your need before Him. And then, thank Him that He is big enough to take care of everything!

DAY 29

THE VERY BEST PLACE TO BE

THERE ARE SOME wonderful places in life—home for Christmas, in a delivery room at the birth of your child, sitting in a concert with your favorite musicians, on the back of a boat watching the sunset across a still lake. Each spot brings its own joy.

But there is simply no better place than God's presence, found in unceasing prayer. The Psalmist recognized this in Psalm, Chapter 84, extolling the glory of being in God's temple in Jerusalem.

For believers now, this symbolizes the thrill of experiencing God in prayerful intimacy every day. Dwelling in His manifest presence. Knowing God in the deepest sense of that term.

The Psalmist says the most blessed man is the man in whose heart are the roadways to this place of intimacy with the LORD God Himself—in "whose heart are the highways to Zion." And look at the treasures he finds!

A LOVELY PLACE

"How lovely is Your dwelling place, O LORD of hosts!"
(Vs. 1)

There simply is no more beautiful environment.

A PLACE TO PURSUE

"My soul longs, yes, faints for the courts of the LORD." *(Vs. 2)*

When we discover the value of God's presence, we desire it more and more.

A PLACE FOR EVERYONE

"Even the sparrow finds a home and the swallow a nest for herself, where she may lay her young, at your altars, O LORD of hosts." (Vs. 3)

None who come to God in humble prayer are turned away.

A PLACE WHERE THE SOVEREIGN KING DWELLS

"O LORD of hosts, my King and my God." (Vs. 3b)

As the sovereign King, He has all authority and power. Every request you have can be provided. Every need met. Nothing is too difficult for an All-Powerful God.

A PLACE OF JOYFUL SINGING AND PRAISE!

"Blessed are those who dwell in your house, ever singing your praise!" (Vs. 4)

Those who dwell in God's presence have the perspective that leads to praise as they see things as they really are.

A PLACE OF INCREASING STRENGTH

"They go from strength to strength. (Vs. 7)

As we make our way deeper and deeper into growing intimacy with Him, we find our strength increasing exponentially.

A PERSONAL PLACE

"...each one appears before God in Zion." (Vs. 7)

Like a father or mother who loves each child the same, God's love is inexhaustibly personal. Every believer who enjoys God's presence is treated individually and finds acceptance, grace, and intimacy as if they were the only one in the world.

A PLACE OF PROTECTION

"For the LORD God is a sun and shield." (Vs. 11)

His presence lights our way, protecting us with each step.

A PLACE OF PROVISION

"No good thing does He withhold from those who walk uprightly." (Vs. 11)

He gladly entrusts His best gifts to those who can be trusted because they are pursuing Him.

A PLACE OF BLESSING

> *"O LORD of hosts, blessed is the one who trusts in You!"*
> *(Vs. 12)*

God's blessing makes the natural, supernatural. The earthly, heavenly. The common, Divine.

SIMPLY THE BEST PLACE POSSIBLE!

> *"For a day in your courts is better than a thousand else-*
> *where. I would rather be a doorkeeper in the house of my*
> *God than dwell in the tents of wickedness." (Vs. 10)*

Where are you choosing to dwell today? In the world's environments or the place of God's presence? Are you entering in through prayer and dwelling there in continual communion with Him, or slogging through the world on your own?

Why settle for a substitute spot when the door to the best place in heaven and earth is open wide?

Pray it in: Spend time in prayer right now, just basking in the beauty of God's presence ... and give Him thanks!

DAY 30

PRAYING FOR FAITH
THROUGH SIFTING

Simon, Simon, behold, Satan has demanded permission to sift you
like wheat; but I have prayed for you, that your faith may not fail;
and you, when once you have turned again, strengthen your
brothers.

(LUKE 22:31-32)

IT HAD BEEN revealed to Jesus that one of His primary disciples, Peter, was going to go through an unusual time of testing. Jesus said that Satan had obtained permission by asking God if he could "sift him like wheat." This is reminiscent of Job, as Satan gained permission to test him. Job went through a similar sifting for a similar purpose.

Sifting wheat was a familiar process to anyone in Peter's culture. Its' design was to remove the chaff—the useless, non-grain that had been gathered in harvest—and to get to the usable wheat. It was vital, but hard work.

WHAT COULD JESUS DO?

Jesus did not say that he would save him from this testing. But what He did say was even more valuable. He said he was praying for him. And, He also indicated that His prayer would be effective.

We think Peter's faith failed, but this would not be Christ's evaluation. It faltered a bit as he denied Christ at a crushing moment when all Peter had hoped and dreamed for—banked his life on—was nailed to a cross.

But, remember that, with John, Peter was the first disciple to the empty tomb! Not many days later, he stands on the day of Pentecost and preaches and, in a single moment, 3,000 people are saved!

His faith had been sifted, as God removed the fluffy, lightweight chaff. But when it returned, he was a lion. Read 1 and 2 Peter and you will find a sobered, matured faith—a faith that was aware and ever vigilant against the enemy and a faith that would stand the test. History tells us that Peter was martyred for his faith. Refusing to be crucified as his Lord, he asked to be crucified upside down.

OUR TASK IN PRAYER

What was Jesus' main responsibility for Peter in this grueling time of testing? To pray, and to pray that Peter's faith would not fail. And, it worked!

What is our responsibility when those we love go through the same season of sifting? We must do the same as Jesus. We must carry them through to a matured faith utilizing the powerful means of effectual prayer!

Who around you is being sifted right now? They could come out on the other side with a damaged faith instead of a developed faith. Their well-being and usefulness for the kingdom may well depend upon your prayers. It may be one of the most important works we ever do in discipling others.

Pray it in: Pray today for someone you know who is being sifted, that their "faith would not fail" and, that "afterward they would strengthen" many others.

DAY 31

WHAT WILL LIFT YOUR SOUL FROM DESPAIR?

Why are you in despair, O my soul? And why have you become disturbed within me? Hope in God, for I shall again praise Him for the help of His presence. O my God, my soul is in despair within me; therefore, I remember You from the land of the Jordan and the peaks of Hermon, from Mount Mizar. Deep calls to deep at the sound of Your waterfalls; all Your breakers and Your waves have rolled over me. The LORD will command His lovingkindness in the daytime, and His song will be with me in the night, a prayer to the God of my life.

(PSALM 42:5-8)

WE ALL FIND ourselves despairing at times. Things don't go right in a relationship or a situation. We lose sight of important things. We err with a sinful choice and then wallow for days in despair because we lose sight of the cross. The possibilities are endless to enter into, what John Bunyan called, the "slough of despond." The question is not, "Why are you in despair, O my soul?" but, "How will you come out of despair, O my soul?" The Psalmist's prayer gives us the answer. And it should become our prayer.

THE HELP OF HIS PRESENCE

The singular solution is the presence of God. Later the Psalmist would proclaim that the "nearness of God is my good" (Psalm 73:28). There is nothing that brings perspective to our problem like the All-Seeing-God. Nothing that gives us the wisdom and confidence to know exactly what to do like the Wonderful Counselor. Nothing that comforts us more than the nearness of the Father. Nothing that grants security like the Lion of the tribe of Judah.

Like a child who has fallen and cries out for his parents, so we must realize there is only one answer for us.

This is why the Psalmist says; "His song will be with me in the night, a prayer to the God of my life." He understood: God alone gives life. He and He alone is what lifts our soul from despair. He is the One to whom we must turn our attention, like a "deer that pants for the water brooks" (Psalm 42:1).

THE FOOLISHNESS OF A SIDEWAYS LOOK

In our pride, we look elsewhere. We think we can manufacture a solution to our despair. That some human device will save us. Some earthly source can be our solution.

Look nowhere else but to Him. No sideways solutions, no silly substitutes. Cultivate the wisdom to run to His presence and seek Him first through His Word, prayer, and the counsel of godly friends filled with God's Word. Have the tunnel vision that looks straightforward to His presence as your only hope and confidence. Pray when you don't feel like it and pray until you do.

Pray until you find yourself engulfed by the God-of-all-Comfort.

And rest assured of this promise: *"The LORD will command His lovingkindness in the daytime; and His song will be with me in the night, a prayer to the God of my life."*

Pray it in: Spend a few minutes in prayerful silence. Reflect on the comfort of God's nearness. Ask God to fill you today with the constant awareness of His presence.

DAY 32

━━━━◅∘C∽୨∘►━━━━

SEEING THE KINGDOM OF GOD COMING WITH POWER!

"If anyone wishes to come after Me, he must deny himself, and take up his cross and follow Me. For whoever wishes to save his life will lose it, but whoever loses his life for My sake and the gospel's will save it." And Jesus was saying to them, "Truly I say to you, there are some of those who are standing here who will not taste death until they see the kingdom of God after it has come with power.

(MARK 8:34-9:1)

DO YOU THINK it's possible? Is there a way we can see the kingdom of God arriving in power? That we can experience what the New Testament believers experienced? That we can see God's kingdom coming and His will being done on earth as it is being done in heaven? Apparently, Jesus thought this was possible, for He gives us clear instructions to take us there.

DENY YOURSELF AND DIE

Jesus gave this unusual pathway to His kingdom's power. Those willing to give their life away would find life indeed. This was a hard saying, calling for surrender to the Master's will. No doubt, Peter, who had watched Roman crucifixions, had a cold chill go up his spine at the thought. He thought following Christ could mean physical death. And he was right, of course. It can.

But in the next breath, Jesus said that those who take up their cross and die would "see the kingdom of God coming with power." What a treasure they would find! What a glory they would experience! Only those who were willing to "lose their life" would find this life. Those who cling to their physical life will never see the kingdom.

TRANSFIGURED

Six days later, Jesus took the inner three disciples up to a mountain and was transfigured before them. Elijah and Moses appeared and had a protracted conversation with Jesus. Peter saw this with his own eyes. It was so recognizable that he named each man.

Take a breath, close your eyes and IMAGINE this moment! These two, great men of God, instantly standing on the hillside as if it were the most common experience, having a nice conversation with the Son of God!

I wonder what they were talking about? Perhaps they were encouraging the man, Jesus, as He made His way to the cross. Moses reminding Jesus how His death would fulfill all the law the Father had given him on Sinai. Elijah, reminding Jesus that his prophecies were all coming true in the next days as he climbed Golgotha.

Peter was seeing exactly what the kingdom of God was like. The kingdom that moves redeemed beings from heaven to earth effortlessly. The kingdom that knows no boundaries. The kingdom where everything the King has said is faithfully fulfilled. The kingdom that has such power that a conversation can occur on a hillside with men who passed from this world, alive and shining and able to converse together.

Suddenly, the whole group was immersed in a cloud of God's glory and they heard God's voice, proclaiming to all that Jesus was His "beloved Son—the Son to whom you should be continually listening." In this kingdom, we can literally hear from the Throne itself! We can hear God and know Him and converse with Him!

This is the kingdom of God. Peter saw it.

THY KINGDOM COME

Immediately following this, a demon-possessed boy was brought to Jesus. The evil spirits inside of him were constantly throwing his helpless body into convulsions. Jesus looked at the people around him and said something about the kingdom: "All things are possible to him who believes." In other words, "There are no boundaries in the kingdom—anything is possible!" With seemingly no exertion, Jesus rebuked the demon and the boy was instantly healed. This is what happens when the "kingdom of God comes in power."

Helping us understand our helplessness to assist such people, and the kingdom power that is available and the way to access it, Jesus sums up the experience this way: "This kind cannot come out by anything but prayer." In other words, "In my kingdom, you can ask God impossible things to help others, and it will be done. For my kingdom transcends the physical laws of this universe. But, it is accessed through prayer."

AND NOW

We are more fortunate than the disciples. Why? We have seen the "kingdom of God come with power." We have seen "greater works," as Jesus prophesied in John, Chapter 14. Not greater in significance, but greater in scope. Jesus' works resulted in 120 disciples at His ascension. Now, His kingdom has advanced to a mighty army of believers, millions upon millions through the ages, advancing across the earth.

The great Vine has spread to a vast vineyard covering the world (John 15:1-2). Miracles happen by the millisecond as people are being ushered into His kingdom by His saving power every hour around the world.

This moment in Jesus' life speaks right to us in our brief experience on this physical planet. Christ's kingdom is coming and His will is being done on earth as it is in heaven.

All who are willing to leave their life behind, follow Him, and pray will see the kingdom of God coming with power!

Pray it in: Where is God calling you to deny yourself and die to your plans and agendas? Spend time wrestling through this before God in prayer, knowing that the kingdom coming in power is at stake.

DAY 33

WHAT REALLY HAPPENS
WHEN YOU PRAY?

WHAT DO YOU do when you and your nation are in serious trouble? When you are in bondage and there seems no way of escape? When you are surrounded by wickedness and evil? When the people of God are in the minority? And, when God's children themselves are unresponsive, sinful, and unrevived?

You PRAY.

Nehemiah, David, Daniel ... go right down the list and you will find their first response was prayer. And their prayers are similar, giving us a model for how we should pray.

FASTING AND PRAYING

Daniel fasted and prayed for 21 days (Daniel, Chapters 9-10). He read his Bible, which stirred and convicted him and prompted him to pray. His prayer was a prayer of confession of his sin and the sins of the people and a cry for mercy.

Read Daniel 9:4-19, and then read Nehemiah, Chapter 1, and you will see that these are almost identical prayers. God heard and answered both.

It was not a momentary prayer. "I went on praying and confessing my sin and the sin of my people, pleading with the Lord my God for Jerusalem, His holy mountain," Daniel said (9:20). It was a continual intercession flowing from a burdened heart.

GOD HEARS PRAYER

"The moment you began praying, a command was given," said Gabriel when he came to speak to Daniel. God sent a messenger to tell Daniel that he was precious to God, (repeated 3 times), and that God had heard his prayers and was going to redeem Israel and send the Messiah in the coming days.

After Daniel prayed, God revealed His will, giving Daniel everything he needed to know about what was ahead. He also encouraged and strengthened Daniel's heart and gave him insight and understanding to lead others.

Amazing things happen when we pray ... and only when we pray. The man who will not give himself to prayer will not be able to see what Daniel saw, nor lead the way Daniel led. They will not have heard from heaven.

NOW WHAT?

So, what should we be doing right now? The same as Daniel, Nehemiah, David and all the great saints who have gone before us.

We must pray. We must confess our sins and the sins of the people. And we must never, never give up.

Pray it in: Spend time praying for the nation. You might want to pray Daniel's prayer in Daniel 9:4-19 or Nehemiah's prayer in Nehemiah, Chapter 1.

DAY 34

THE EFFECTIVENESS OF PRAYER

Therefore He said that He would destroy them, had not Moses His chosen one stood in the breach before Him, to turn away His wrath from destroying them.

(PSALM 106:23)

THERE ARE SOME who choose a lifelong path in prayer. But, sadly, there are some professing believers who rarely ever pray. They do not comprehend what they are missing. They are trying to navigate a stifling world without spiritual oxygen.

OUR GREAT PRIVILEGE

Non-praying believers—if they are believers at all—fail to realize the incredible opportunity they have been granted. Like Moses, we can "stand in the breach before God." Like no others, we can approach God's throne to find "grace to help in time of need."

Prayer can do whatever God can do, for prayer brings God into the equation. If we neglect this privilege, we will one day regret that we laid aside our greatest work, which would have led to our greatest effectiveness and joy. We will be appalled that we spent so many of our days in frivolous things.

OUR GREAT RESPONSIBILITY

As redeemed ones, we now have the means to aid in the rescue of others, like Moses. We can go before God on their behalf. God not only welcomes this intercession but invites it. He tells us to pray without ceasing. Why would he demand such an activity if it were useless? If it accomplished nothing? If there were not things He longed to achieve through us in the loop of Divine intercession?

God is ever training His children to rule and reign for eternity, and part of our training is to learn how to pray. How to remain in communion for others out of love for them and faith in God. How to persevere without wavering. How to find God. How to bank on His promises. How to engage in the eternal work.

Prayer is not something for a few privileged believers. It is our responsibility as children of God to use this mighty tool for the salvation of others and the glory of God. Even the newest, youngest believer can pray and be heard by our all-powerful God!

OUR GREAT POWER

God has repeatedly told us that there is an efficacy in prayer. That it works. That the "fervent prayer of a righteous man accomplishes much" (James 5:16).

What if we *believed* this? All of us? What if a nation full of God's children stood in the breach before God for the people of our land to "turn away His wrath from destroying them?" What if all the people of God would cry out for sweeping revival in the church and spiritual awakening among unbelievers? What if we joined in intercession for a tidal wave of God's presence so that "the earth would be full of the knowledge of the Lord like waters that cover the sea?" (Habakkuk 2:14).

What if God found us interceding for His Bride, the Church, that she would be cleansed and purified and expanded for His glory? Would He refuse a prayer like this? Or, would He grant those requests as He did for a faithful intercessor named Moses?

And what if history was changed because of our faithfulness in prayer?

And, what if we began today?

Pray it in: Will you spend time standing in the gap for someone you love right now? Consider fasting and praying on their behalf this week.

DAY 35

YOU'RE MORE CAPABLE THAN YOU THINK

ALL OF US wonder if we have what it takes to make a difference. Will our life count? Will we reach our God-given potential? Will we do what we were designed and created to do?

Not without *prayer*.

Prayer connects us to God and moves the hand of God. God has ordained that His highest creations unite with Him through Christ's saving work and His Spirit's indwelling. Through the daily practice of communion with Him in His Word and prayer, we join with Him in a partnership that unleashes His power through us.

With prayer—unceasing, fervent prayer—as the foundation of our lives, EVERYTHING is possible! James assures us of a phenomenal promise.

> *The effective prayer of a righteous man can accomplish much. (James 5:16)*

There it is. Our pathway to accomplishing great things for God. When we DON'T pray we get what man can do; when we DO

PRAY we get what God can do ... in our life, our family, our church, our ministry, in our witness to those far from God.

It is almost as if James thinks we won't believe this and so he reminds us that this promise is for any common follower of Christ. (This is about YOU!)

> *Elijah was a man **with a nature like ours**, and he prayed earnestly that it would not rain, and it did not rain on the earth for three years and six months. Then he prayed again, and the sky poured rain and the earth produced its fruit. (Vs. 17-18, emphasis mine)*

He also reminds us in this same chapter of the ultimate purpose of this partnership while we are on earth. It is so people wandering from Him can be brought home. The tool of God-empowered intercession is for the purpose of helping people God loves to come to repentance and faith. He wants to continually, exponentially expand the work of Christ to "take away the sins of the world." And He wants to use us in the process.

> *My brethren, if any among you strays from the truth and one turns him back, let him know that he who turns a sinner from the error of his way will save his soul from death and will cover a multitude of sins. (Vs. 19-20)*

Do you want to accomplish something eternal today? Get your heart right with God, pray all day long for others, and follow the Spirit's promptings as He leads you in loving testimony to all as He directs. Then stand back and see what a mighty God will do through a praying servant!

Pray it in: Spend time in believing prayer right now for people God has placed in your life that are far from God.

DAY 36

—∘✦∘—

HEAVEN OPENING

While He was praying, heaven was opened.

(*LUKE 3:21*)

THE BAPTISM OF Jesus was a remarkable, not-to-be-repeated event. Jesus came, like the sinners he was about to save, to submit to John for baptism. This act announced His identification with the Father and the beginning of His public ministry. Also, He was setting a pattern for everyone who would follow Him.

But do not miss the simple phrase, "while He was praying." Why does Luke record this simple travelogue? Why was He praying? Jesus, as a man, is modeling for us exactly how we are to live. Here He reminds us again that we are to pray without ceasing ... to live every moment in the conscious awareness of communion with the Father. I would imagine that it was not only for instruction, but the desire for simple, pure, loving communion that Jesus talked so constantly to His Father.

HEAVEN OPENING

But on this occasion of public obedience and prayer, something extraordinary happened: "Heaven was opened."

What does this signify? We cannot fully know as Luke records it for us. I wonder if, at this moment, God had something that could only be done with an open heaven? He sent His Spirit in full measure and gave His blessing and commission in audible form. It was the enduement of the Spirit for service and the announcement that this was the One—above all others—who had the full blessing and favor of the Father. This was no ordinary man. What Jesus was and did blessed the Father fully.

Or, perhaps it was simply that the Father and Spirit wanted to come in greater display just to make known that they were one with the Son. This would validate Christ's ministry before a watching world. I even wonder if God was bursting with such overwhelming joy at this moment, that it called for a visible, audible expression of His glory. Like a proud father rushing on the football field to cheer on his son. This was God's Son—His only begotten Son—and the joy of the Father exploded in perfect pride and special gifts.

One thing is for sure: such a man—with the full measure of the Spirit and full blessing of the Father—is worth following.

But also, for Jesus Himself this moment was unique. He had obeyed God in baptism and this manifestation happened "while He was praying." The heavens opened for a special blessing from the Father.

HEAVENS OPENING NOW

All of us who follow Christ have had moments when God was unusually present. Special movements of God are times when God "rends the heavens" and comes down (Isaiah 64:1). Heaven opens. What can explain 15% of the population in America in the First Great Awakening coming to Christ in just a few years? Do the math on your town and see what that phenomena would mean. It is unusual. Spectacular. An open heaven.

But don't forget ... it happened while He was praying. Do you want an open heaven over your life and your church and our nation? Then it's time to pray.

Pray it in: Make this your prayer:

> "*Lord, deliver me from a merely human life. I long for more of You. More of Your presence; more of Your power. I need You, Lord. Would you open heaven over my life, my family, my church, our community? Would you rend the heavens and come down? And as you bless us, would you remind us that only One should receive the glory?*"

HOW HUNGRY ARE YOU FOR GOD?

IF YOU STUDY the things of God and observe His people, you quickly realize there is a dividing line. There are some men and women to whom God is peripheral and others to whom He is central and all-consuming.

The former experience the Divine Presence occasionally—the latter, often and deeply. Those who find Him often are the ones who move us as we read their stories and hear their prayers.

This is why David, the Sweet Psalmist of Israel, left a legacy that blesses millions. To read His Psalms is to hear the heart of a man who is consumed with God—always hungry for more, always turning in God's direction, always crying out, and always finding and experiencing the depths of God.

God's evaluation of David was that he was a "man after (My) own heart" (1 Samuel 13:14). This indicates that in spite of his faults and failings, David was in constant pursuit of God. He was not after his agenda, but God's—His glory, but the Father's.

Psalm, Chapter 143, consists of only 12 verses. But as we dissect it, we discover all that David is doing that indicates His longing for God. And most of all, we see the things He is asking God to do in prayer.

HIS HONEST CONFESSION

David had a serious problem. He evaluates his situation well and lays it out before God. He doesn't try to "pull himself up by his own bootstraps" or manage the problems of his life by himself. He doesn't stuff them or ignore them. He honestly admits his situation and spreads the dilemma before the only One who can help.

- *The enemy has persecuted my soul (Vs. 3)*

- *He has crushed my life to the ground (Vs. 3)*

- *He has made me dwell in dark places (Vs. 3)*

- *My spirit is overwhelmed within me (Vs. 4)*

- *My heart is appalled within me (Vs. 4)*

HIS HUMBLE RESPONSE

But David is not passive. He's not simply moaning before God. His was a confession of need and a cry of aggressive faith. He is looking, remembering, stretching out, trusting, turning to God. His is not a thought of "nobody can help me" or, "there's nothing I can do." He is not merely whining, but pursuing God with vigorous passion. And he pursues Him in prayer. Notice the verbs in his prayer.

- *I **remember** the days of old (Vs. 5)*

- *I **meditate** on all Your doings (Vs. 5)*

- *I **muse** on the work of Your hands (Vs. 5)*

- *I **stretch out** my hands to You (Vs. 6)*

- *My soul **longs** for you (Vs. 5)*

- *I **trust** in You (Vs. 8)*

- *To You I **lift up** my soul (Vs. 8)*

- *I **take refuge** in You (Vs. 9)*

- *You are my God (Vs. 10)*

- *I am Your servant (Vs. 12)*

HIS HEARTFELT CRY

With the confidence of a child who believes in His faithful Father, He prays. He assumes God will answer because of the perfection of His character. He appeals to God's faithfulness, righteousness, and lovingkindness. He prays for a reviving of His soul "for the sake of Your Name, O Lord." And his cry is intense and specific. He is asking, which is exactly what the Lord has commanded us to unashamedly do.

- ***Hear** my prayer (Vs. 1)*

- ***Give ear** to my supplications (Vs. 1)*

- ***Answer me** in Your faithfulness (Vs. 1)*

- ***Do not enter into judgment** with Your servant (Vs. 2)*

- ***Answer me** quickly, O Lord (Vs. 7)*

- ***Do not hide your face** from me (Vs. 7)*

- *Let me hear Your lovingkindness* in the morning *(Vs. 8)*

- *Teach me* the way in which I should walk *(Vs. 8)*

- *Deliver me*, O Lord, from my enemies *(Vs. 9)*

- *Teach me* to do Your will *(Vs. 10)*

- Let Your good Spirit *lead me* on level ground *(Vs. 10)*

- For the sake of Your name ... *revive me (Vs. 11)*

- In Your righteousness *bring my soul out of trouble (Vs. 11)*

- In Your lovingkindness, *cut off my enemies (Vs. 12)*

- *Destroy all those* who afflict my soul *(Vs. 12)*

The most beautiful thing is that David was heard. God did answer—over and over again. And David experienced depths of God that most of us never know, simply because he prayed with honest confession and bold faith.

Why would we not, right now, pursue Him with similar honesty, humility, and heartfelt intercession? If we do, we will find that the God of David will answer us. We will become men and women who are "after God's own heart," like David. And we will experience the same mighty, reviving God.

Pray it in: Spend time praying through Psalm 143. Make it your prayer.

DAY 38

WHEN GOD WILL NOT HEAR OUR CRY

(OR, THE ROLE OF REPENTANCE IN REVIVAL)

*They have turned back to the iniquities of their ancestors who refused to hear My words, and they have gone after other gods to serve them; the house of Israel and the house of Judah have broken My covenant which I made with their fathers. Therefore, thus says the Lord, "Behold I am bringing disaster on them which they will not be able to escape; **though they will cry to Me, yet I will not listen to them."** Then the cities of Judah and the inhabitants of Jerusalem will go and cry to the gods to whom they burn incense, but they surely will not save them in the time of their disaster.*

(JEREMIAH 11:10-12, *emphasis mine*)

GOD HEARS OUR prayers. This is one of the great truths of the Bible—a truth upon which we deeply rely. And, in this particular season in our nation, a truth that we desperately must understand and apply.

But is there a possibility of crying out and God not hearing and delivering? A deaf ear from the only One who can save us?

WHEN GOD TURNS A DEAF EAR

When the judgment of God comes it is for the intent of our turning. It is like pain to the human body to awaken us to something we are doing that is hurting us and others. It is a call to understand our sin and humbly return to the God who made us. To live once again by "every word that proceeds from the mouth of God."

But what if God sends his remedial judgment, (judgment designed to bring us to a remedy), and we will not repent? We won't turn? We keep following after the gods of this world?

Apparently at that moment, God will *not* hear and answer our prayers. This makes perfect sense. If the purpose of discipline is not heeded, the discipline must continue.

THE PRAYER GOD HEARS

Humble, repentant prayers will be heard and answered. But make no mistake: the One who reigns over all will ignore proud, unrepentant prayers.

Is God calling for repentance in some area of our lives? Our church? Our community? Our nation? We cannot ignore His work and expect a response. Our disobedience to His given Word will always quench His Spirit.

God is not playing games. He does not speak to be disregarded. Do we want to be heard? Then we must listen to God's evaluation and direction. We must have a willing heart to do what He desires and then cry out to Him. He will hear every humble, repentant cry!

Pray it in: Pray this simple prayer of David, "Search me, O God, and know my heart. Try me and know my anxious thoughts and see if there be any hurtful way in me and lead me in the everlasting way" (Psalm 139:23-24). As God directs, confess and repent of your sin.

DAY 39

WHAT IF I'VE GIVEN UP?

(OR, CAN MY CRY MAKE A DIFFERENCE?)

TO GAZE AROUND us and see the devastation of ruined walls in every direction in our nation is overwhelming. Often we think there is simply nothing we can do. Our feeble efforts bring a quick rise of response, but no seeming lasting change. If we are not careful, creeping doubt will damage our faith to the extent that we wonder if prayer will matter at all.

> *"Our struggle is—isn't it?—to achieve and retain faith on a lower level. To believe that there is a Listener at all. For as the situation grows more and more desperate, the grisly fears intrude. Are we only talking to ourselves in an empty universe?" (C.S. Lewis, "Letters to Malcolm, Chiefly on Prayer")*

But even a cursory glance through human history reveals God's immutable promises. He has bound Himself in this age to certain reliabilities. And, one of those is His faithfulness to our humble, believing cries. He whispers through the sweet stories of humble men and women who simply relied on Him. And He shouts through His prophets.

THE WILLINGNESS OF HIS CHARACTER

What binds God is Himself. He cannot deny His nature because He is ever true to who He is. The compassion of His heart is overwhelming and so He exercises a patience that is beyond anything humans can comprehend.

> *Therefore, the Lord longs to be gracious to you, and therefore He waits on high to have compassion on you. For the Lord is a God of justice. How blessed are all those who long for Him. (Isaiah 30:18)*

THE STATED PROMISE REGARDING OUR PRAYERS

What is most amazing is that the slightest, humble turn of our heart will take us right to Him. He is peering over heaven to hear and has bound Himself to answer.

> *"He will surely be gracious to you at the sound of your cry; when He hears it, He will answer you." (Isaiah 30:19)*

And when He enters the equations of our lives, He brings overwhelming change, and it can happen in an instant. Provision, vision, direction, clarity, release from the bondage of the gods of this world—all these things and more come flowing from His presence.

> *Although the Lord has given you bread of privation and*

water of oppression, He, your Teacher will no longer hide Himself, but your eyes will behold your Teacher. Your ears will hear a word behind you, "This is the way, walk in it," whenever you turn to the right or to the left. And you will defile your graven images overlaid with silver, and your molten images plated with gold. You will scatter them as an impure thing, and say to them, "Be gone!" (Isaiah 30:20-22)

Our prayers make a difference. He WILL hear our cry ... and He is waiting right now!

Pray it in: Pray for our nation right now. Pray in faith, knowing that God will hear and answer your prayer, just as He has done in the past. Be encouraged as you realize there are millions around the country who are joining you in prayer!

THE TRAVAIL THAT PRECEDES SPIRITUAL AWAKENING

In 1927, my grandad, A.P. Elliff, went to be the pastor of First Baptist Church in Lavaca, Arkansas. In that day, Lavaca was a small farming community outside Ft. Smith with just a few hundred people in the entire town.

Grandad and his wife, Sue, and two kids (one was my dad) were coming from South Arkansas and had to wait a week to let the Arkansas River subside so the ferry could cross. The 1927 flood was the most devastating in Arkansas history, destroying entire towns. In some places, the water stood 30 feet deep for months.

The Mississippi, in certain junctures, was over 60 miles wide, sending water back into Arkansas rivers, along with the torrential rain. The White River flowed backward because of the rush of water from the Mississippi. Hundreds died in its path up and down the river, but the greatest devastation was in Arkansas.

THE MEETING

Every year, when the crops were laid by, the church planned a two-week revival. In fact, they would meet until God came.

There is no doubt that the tragedy of the flood lay deeply in the people's minds as they planned for the annual meeting in August 1927 with their new pastor.

A.P. was glad to be asked to lead the meeting in his new church of less than 100 people. He reconfigured the little church so more people could fit in the white frame building. He took out the windows so they could get better ventilation in the August heat.

THE TRAVAIL

The meeting was going well with a few here and there coming to Christ. But my Dad remembers, as a young boy, hearing my Grandad and Grandmother in the parlor of their little parsonage, praying every night. "The revival hasn't broken," he heard Grandad say. "We must pray more."

A few nights later, God gave my Grandad a verse from Isaiah, that he specifically felt was for the moment.

"When Zion travails, sons and daughters will be born unto her." (Isaiah 66:8)

He went before the small congregation and asked them to come an hour early each night to labor in prayer ... and they did. As the prayer increased, so did the crowds. Flatbed wagons were brought in and placed outside the windows for seating. The building was packed as news of God's movement spread across the region. Hundreds came, and many were saved.

A few weeks later, 1725 people attended the baptism. There were 142 cars carrying 994 people, 58 wagons with 480 people, 3 flatbed trucks with 75 people, 6 buggies with 12 people, 10 people came on horseback, and 50 on foot. (My grandad meticulously recorded the details, so all the glory would go to God!)

At the end of the meeting, my Grandad wrote in his diary: "108 people baptized in 68 minutes in Vash Gash creek" as God brought spiritual awakening to an entire community ... when the people of Zion travailed in prayer.

THE PRICE

There are many components that go into such a season of spiritual harvest. The bold proclamation of the gospel, people inviting others to come into a gospel gathering (this is still one of God's methods, by the way.) And, most importantly, the Divine, gracious working of our saving God.

But no such movement ever occurs, it seems, without the travail of the church. Such spiritual labor is the birth pangs of awakening.

What would happen, in your city, if every church had such an outpouring? In Central Arkansas where I serve, if every church had a similar work of God it would mean over 65,000 people coming to Christ within a month. We must not laugh at this possibility, for God has done this before. Regularly, in fact, in seasons of great revival and spiritual awakening.

We long for such movement, but will we pay the price in preparation, proclamation, and travailing prayer?

Will we pray *with no intermission*?

Pray it in: Would you spend a significant time in prayer today? Ask God to make you a person who prays without ceasing—all day, every day. Let these 40 days be a beginning, not an end to a more vibrant prayer life.

Then rise tomorrow, read your regular Bible reading and look for what God is saying to you. After your reading, **Pray it in!** Take the truth of the Scripture and spend time in prayer asking it to become true in your life and the lives of those around you.

Let this 40-day adventure become a lifelong journey in prayer. God is waiting for you today, and every day. Will you walk with Him and let Him teach you how to pray with no intermission?

APPENDIX

For further reading on prayer ...

Old Paths, New Power (*Daniel Henderson*)

Transforming Prayer (*Daniel Henderson*)

Prayer (*O. Hallesby*)

A Passion for Prayer (*Tom Elliff*)

Fresh Wind, Fresh Fire! (*Jim Cymbala*)

Breakthrough Prayer (*Jim Cymbala*)

Prayer (*Timothy Keller*)

The Concert of Prayer (*Bob Bakke*)

The Power of Extraordinary Prayer (*Bob Bakke*)

Prayer: Communing with God in Everything (*A. W. Tozer*)

The Complete Work of E.M. Bounds (*E. M. Bounds*)

With Christ in the School Prayer (*Andrew Murray*)

The Power of Prayer and Fasting (*Ronnie Floyd*)

Prayer on Fire (*Fred Hartley*)

Studies on the Sermon on the Mount (*Martyn Lloyd-Jones, Read the section on the Lord's Prayer especially. It is life-changing.*)

The Kneeling Christian (*Anonymous*)

Prayer Power Unlimited (*J. Oswald Sanders*)

Pray Like it Matters (*Steve Gaines*)

Additional writings by Bill Elliff

Graceful truth Series

The Line of Faith
40 Days to Deepened Dependency

The Essential Presence
40 Days to Increased Intimacy

Books

One Cry
A Nationwide Call to Spiritual Awakening
Byron Paulus and Bill Elliff

The Presence-Centered Church

Whitewater
Navigating the Rapids of Church Conflict

Simply Prayer
Joining God for the Rest of Your Life

Children's Books

The Child of 10,000 Names

The Christmas Tree Story
Scott Edge and Bill Elliff

BOOKLETS

Forgiveness
Healing the Harbored Hurts of Your Heart

Lifting Life's Greatest Load
How to Gain and Maintain a Clear Conscience

Having MORE Kids Who Follow Christ
Holly Elliff and Bill Elliff

Everyman

The Power and Joy of Biblical Fasting

PAMPHLETS

50 Marks of a Man of God
Spiritual Evaluation for Leaders

Personal Revival Checklist
Spiritual Evaluation from the Sermon on the Mount

To order additional books go to:
www.billelliff.org/store

Made in the USA
Monee, IL
28 August 2020

38907702R00079